WRITING VIOLENCE AND BUDDHISM IN SRI LANKA

This book examines the idea of violence in the context of religion and literature. It addresses the question of freedom and peace, and violence, with reference to the Buddhist nationalist discourse in Sri Lanka, against the backdrop of Shyam Selvadurai's novel *The Hungry Ghosts*. The book discusses love, compassion, emancipation, ethics, and responsibility through the concepts of identity, deconstruction, and decolonization to view religion as language or writing. With a blend of philosophical insights from Emmanuel Levinas, Jacques Derrida, Maurice Blanchot, and Mahatma Gandhi on ideas of being and the other, differences, nonviolence and forgiveness, it insists on the ethical exigency of reinventing Buddhism in Sri Lanka. Delving into some of the central motifs of Selvadurai's novel, such as suffering, desire, hate, and vengeance, it questions popular Sinhala Buddhist readings to argue for the promise of inclusive and diverse approaches towards various groups, linguistic communities, women, and homosexuality.

This book will be useful for scholars and researchers of literature and languages, South Asian literature, literary criticism and theory, linguistics, cultural studies, philosophy, religion, Buddhist studies, diaspora studies, and Sri Lankan literature and sociology.

Nimmi N. Menike is Senior Lecturer, Department of Language Studies, Faculty of Humanities and Social Sciences, The Open University of Sri Lanka. She was Fellow at the Indian Institute of Advanced Study, Shimla, India, for two years, and completed her PhD from Jawaharlal Nehru University, New Delhi. Her research informs on language and literature in addressing violence in the context of constructing identities. She also volunteers at Daham Pahana, a charitable trust in Sri Lanka.

WRITING VIOLENCE AND BUDDHISM IN SRI LANKA

Of Hungry Ghosts and Homecomings

Nimmi N. Menike

LONDON AND NEW YORK

First published 2022
by Routledge
4 Park Square, Milton Park, Abingdon, Oxon OX14 4RN

and by Routledge
605 Third Avenue, New York, NY 10158

Routledge is an imprint of the Taylor & Francis Group, an informa business

British Library Cataloguing-in-Publication Data
A catalogue record for this book is available from the British Library

Library of Congress Cataloging-in-Publication Data
A catalog record has been requested for this book

ISBN: 978-0-367-48180-3 (hbk)
ISBN: 978-1-032-23313-0 (pbk)
ISBN: 978-1-003-04521-2 (ebk)

DOI: 10.4324/9781003045212

Typeset in Sabon
by Deanta Global Publishing Services, Chennai, India

TO *AMMA*, FOR HER UNCONDITIONAL LOVE
..., AND TO *APPACHCHI* FOR WHO HE IS...

CONTENTS

ACKNOWLEDGEMENTS

These chapters bloomed in Shimla at yet another point where language broke. It breaks mostly at unexpected points, places, and moments, like how it happens in life. It is this vulnerability in/of language as well as of being which appears through these pages, these letters, these writings.

However, these thoughts and writings could appear in the form of a book only because of the in-residence two-year research fellowship granted to me by the Indian Institute of Advanced Study, Shimla, Himachal Pradesh, India. I would like to acknowledge my debts to the Institute. I am deeply thankful to the then Director, Prof. Makarand R. Paranjape, not only for his generous support extended to me as a fellow throughout the two years, but also for his erudite scholarship through which I was exposed to the Gandhian thought of non-violence and to the idea of "colorful cosmopolitanism." This excellent place for research had become home to me, especially because of the caring staff at the Institute, who were always ready with their helping hand to make the stay comfortable and trouble-free.

I convey my gratitude to Prof. Franson Manjali, my PhD supervisor, who delivered me to a world consoled by the thoughts of Jacques Derrida and Maurice Blanchot; to Prof. Manidipa Sen for her love, care, and hospitality. Their presence in all aspects of my life is remarkable.

My special acknowledgement-cum-thanks to Shyam Selvadurai, the writer of *The Hungry Ghosts*, for his generosity.

My heartiest thanks to Brother Charles, the founder of Daham Pahana, for taking me on a spiritual journey. I am also thankful to my Yoga teacher Ms. Gayatri Iyer. The magical touch of her Yoga techniques was, still is, the key to staying focused, balanced, and at peace. I appreciate the help I received from my colleagues at the Department of Language Studies, Faculty of Social Sciences and Humanities, The Open University of Sri Lanka, Nawala. While writing these chapters, I enjoyed the motherly affection of Prof. Anitha and the beautiful friendship of Sanjay Kaushal, Wasanthi Hemamali, Amrita Banerjee, Anne Hartig, Piyali Majumdar, Enakshi Nandi, and Anjali Dulhan. Dicky Thaththi is a blessing in my life. I cannot forget the support of Dr. Sarath Vitharana, who directed me to India for my doctoral studies. I like to recall the beautiful conversations on literature, democracy, and Derrida that I had with Dr. Athula Samarakoon at JNU's Ganga Dhaba.

I acknowledge and thank Penguin India and the Westwood Creative Artists for granting me permission to quote the lines from *The Hungry Ghosts*. I am truly grateful to Shoma Choudhury and Rimina Mohapatra from Routledge India for their tireless support throughout the publication procedure. My sincere thanks to R. Narayanan, the copyeditor, from Deanta Global.

Finally, I thank my parents, my brother, and sister-in-law for their love and understanding, as well as Chanula, Sageeth, and Methula for their warmth.

INTRODUCTION

This work attempts to understand how we, as humans, consciously or unconsciously accommodate and consent to violence against the other while addressing our desire for ownership or belongingness. This desire, which is always a desire for the self operative both individually and collectively, is often, if not always, unaware of the potential harm that it carries within unless it is kept under constant vigil by the one who bears it—*to bear* also means "to carry, to put up with, to stomach, to suffer, to tolerate, to accept, to contain, to hold, to wear, and to expect" it (Menike 2020, 250). It may hurt or injure another. Therefore, before questioning the *other's* desires, every human should question *his/her* desire to realize whether it could harm another. In such an effort to be sincerely made going by one's conscience, one singularly ruminates how to define violence in an impartial or unbiased manner. This deliberation enables one to understand how he/she intentionally or unintentionally participates, contributes, and consents to violence. Insisting on the urgency of understanding our hypocrisy in the act of defining *what* violence *is*, French philosopher Marc Crépon opens his latest work, *Murderous Consent: On Accommodation of Violent Death*, with the following introductory paragraph.

> No critique of violence, no denunciation of cruelty, to the extent that both the one and the other are partial [partiel] and partisan [partial], can elude the risk of consenting, actively or passively, implicitly or explicitly, to the very violence it critiques and cruelty it denounces. It suffices that the critique apply only to violence and the denunciation only to cruelty that take place elsewhere and otherwise. This is the paradox of every protest and every expression of indignation, whether moral or political. No matter how legitimate our protestations may be, the silence, the incomprehension, the small and not-so-small concessions regarding the various forms of violent death that they imply or tolerate, which weave the fabric of our history, compromise death's meaning and their import. As

 DOI: 10.4324/9781003045212-1

> soon as such protestation accept or even draw a line of (political, ideological, economic, military, or individual) separation between people whose wounds are judged unacceptable and people whose sufferings might be seen as tenable, they expose their lack of coherence with the principles they espouse. As soon as such protestations find "good" reasons here for the destructions that they condemn elsewhere, they lose their essential credibility, unless we conclude that violence is natural and has primacy over considerations of ethics. We cannot, in other words, claim for some what we refuse to others. Our awareness of violence and its effects cannot depend on the affiliation of those who suffer, no matter how that affiliation is defined, whether geographically, "ethnically", "factionally", "culturally", politically, or religiously.
>
> (Crépon 2019, 1–2)

Therefore, any sincere effort aiming *to discuss* the question of violence should firstly be aware of the same (effort) having the tendency of becoming double standard in approach. It should struggle to guard itself against this tendency of becoming biased, partial, or inclined because of some fear and worry of losing whatsoever recognition that one had already earned socially, politically, religiously, professionally, or culturally. In other words, the question of violence could be addressed only if one attempts to detach his/herself from the desire for belongingness—the discourse of identity. In that sense, any sincere endeavour attempted for non-violence while struggling to deal with the question of violence is an infinite conversation that unfolds between self and the other. Here, when I say other, it could be the one either inside me or anterior to me. As Derrida argues, "the absolute other in myself or the absolute other outside amounts to the same thing" (Brannigan 1996, 222). *If* and *when* one fails to self-engage in such conversation, violence erupts in unimaginable forms and manners. Though there are innumerable examples, which communicate either the human reluctance to initiate such engaging conversation or the collapse of a dialogue started off to avoid or lessen committing violence against the other, the present work takes some of those from post-independent Sri Lanka as the backdrop of this discussion focused on violence.

Sri Lanka and Violence

The concern of this work on violence in post-independent Sri Lanka echoes the question noted by Sri Lankan anthropologist, Stanley Jeyaraja Tambiah in *Buddhism Betrayed?: Religion, Politics, and Violence in Sri Lanka* (1992). The question I am going to write here quoting Tambiah is the one posed to him by his "colleagues, friends, and acquaintances" while travelling in the USA. The question is, "If Buddhism preaches nonviolence, why is there so much political violence in Sri Lanka today?" (Ibid, 1). In Tambiah's words, the question is "discomfiting." Yet, no matter how embarrassing it may sound, such questions should appear more than once interrupting the flow of dominant discourses operative in terms of religion, ethnicity, nation, and so on, for they help us see the flaws of those discourses, which are otherwise projected to be flawless.

As Tambiah writes, there are several ways to respond to this question. One way is to pose the same question to the interrogator by changing the proper nouns in the question and to make the others see the problems in their own discourses. That would be a way to shut not the question but the one who asks it, for the question remains even in silence. However, recalling the possibilities that he could have employed to give a befitting answer to the question posed, he says,

> I could reply that although Christianity preaches brotherly love, Catholics and Protestants are killing each other in Northern Ireland, or that despite Gandhi's advocacy of *ahimsa* (nonviolence) and *satyagraha* (renunciation of coercion), there is much religious and ethnic violence in India. This is not a helpful reply, but one that temporarily puts the questioner on the defensive. Furthermore, it carries the cynical implication that religion is merely an epiphenomenon and has little impact on realpolitik.
>
> (Ibid)

Hence, he takes a different approach to explore this question by probing the manner in which Buddhism espoused by Sri Lankans of the late 19th and 20th centuries has contributed to the ethnic conflict and violence in Sri Lanka. If it has contributed, as he raises, "were there changes in the nature of that contribution over time? And if there have been changes, how are we to describe the changing or changed shape of Buddhism as a lived reality?" (Ibid, 2).

The question posed to Tambiah and the questions consequently raised by Tambiah highlight one point, that is, violence in Buddhist Sri Lanka. Whenever we hear this phrase, *violence in Buddhist Sri Lanka*, the first thing it reminds us is the ethnic conflict between Sri Lankan Sinhalese and Tamils stretched for almost three decades and finally officially ended in May 2009 with the death of the Liberation of Tamil Eelam (LTTE) leader Velupillai Prabhakaran. The difficulty in reading, understanding, and defining this end as a *victory* pushed some to the edges of language to find some good words to name the event of death(s) in 2009—the military success gained by the state.

If this war between the majority Sinhalese and the minority Tamils could be seen *only* as an issue of political violence, the question that Tambiah encountered in the USA would have been different. Then, the first part of the question concerned with Buddhism, "if Buddhism preaches nonviolence," certainly would not have appeared, and the question would not have become "discomfiting." Even if it does, it would have been different. Here, what is embarrassing is involving Buddhism in state violence. In that sense, it is not a question of *political violence* in the country but one that puts religion in question because of the connection of Buddhism to violence. Such connection is unimaginable (not because of the mindfulness of Sri Lankans to spare Buddhism from state politics) because of Buddhism being a religion espousing non-violence. However, in the present context, it is Sri Lankan Buddhism that is in question as it is dragged into Sri Lankan state politics, projecting it as a reason to fight with non-Buddhists, namely the Hindus, Muslims, and the Christians in the country. On the other hand, there is a growing tendency to justify violence *if* and *when* done to protect and save Buddhism in the country.

Now, this situation, like many other situations happening in the world *in the name of* religion, makes us wonder why people fight at all to save religion, which is, otherwise, to save people from fighting. Moreover, even if people could fight for anything, including religion, is there a *religious* way of justifying violence? These two questions yield our serious attention until we come up with some tenable solution that emphasizes the meaninglessness in fighting *for* religion and seeking *religious* justification *for* violence. In such arduous yet unavoidable responsibility, insights of Gandhi as a sociopolitical, economic, and cultural reformer of recent times hold utmost significance since they help us understand whether there *could be* as well as whether there *should be* any religious justification to violence. His profound thinking on *Mahabharata*, in which his reflection on the *Gita* appears, is one of the best examples, which communicates how he perceived the great epic and made the best sense out of it. It is as follows:

> Even in 1888–9, when I first became acquainted with the Gita, I felt that it was not an historical work, but that, under the guise of physical warfare, it described the duel that perpetually went on in the hearts of mankind, and that physical warfare was brought in merely to make the description of the internal duel more alluring. This preliminary intuition became more confirmed on a closer study of religion and the Gita. A study of the Mahabharata gave it added confirmation. I do not regard the Mahabharata as historical work in the accepted sense. The Adiparva contains powerful evidence in support of my opinion. By ascribing to the chief actors superhuman of subhuman origins, the great Vyasa made short work of the history of kings and their peoples. The persons therein described may be historical, *but the author of the Mahabharata has used them merely to drive home his religious theme.*

> *The author of the Mahabharata has not established the necessity of physical warfare; on the contrary he has proved its futility. He has made the victors shed tears of sorrow and repentance, and has left them nothing but a legacy of miseries.*
>
> (Duncan, Selected Writings, 29,. italics added)

Gandhi's singular approach to *Mahabharata* insists on the inability to find any religious justification of violence even if it is committed only to protect one's community identified by religion, race, clan, caste, class, gender, nation, language, and so on. Now, this idea of Gandhi is accordant with the Buddhist idea of non-violence—the concept of *ahimsa*, which demands very sincere self-determination to be ethically responsible to the other when pursuing self-happiness and freedom. Self-responsibility to the other is fundamental to the Buddhist idea of non-violence.[1] Five precepts of Buddhism to be followed by the laity every day suggest the responsibility to non-violence.[2] Neither a tradition nor a sect identified with Buddhism[3] could turn a blind eye to the very fundamental on which it is founded—*ahimsa*. If one becomes a Buddhist by claiming to be so, then that claim undeniably bears this promise of responsibility to non-violence and, thereby, to be ethically concerned on how one uses his/her *ability* to be(come) the *power* and the *powerful* in the relationship between self and the other.

However, Buddhism unfolding in post-independent Sri Lanka shows a stark difference when compared with the one which emerged in ancient India during the 5th century BCE. This, however, does not mean that early Buddhism was completely absolved of violence, for such absoluteness is impossible (Derrida 2002) to any religion because the founding moment of each religion introduces a rupture in socio-religious-cultural, and political, as well as economic discourses *already* existed. Nevertheless, the point to be highlighted here is the degree of violence committed *in* and *under the name* of Buddhism is soaring today in Sri Lanka to the extent that the fundamentals of Buddhism based on non-violence have begun to recede drastically.

Considering the scenario in contemporary Sri Lanka, it is necessary to understand that the propensity for such violence against non-Buddhists in the country, Hindus, Christians, and Muslims, is a consequence of Sinhala Buddhist revivalism kindled by Anagarika Dharmapala in the latter part of 19th-century Sri Lanka (Kemper 1991; Gombrich and Obyesekere 1988; Obeyesekere 2018). Commenting on the present-day Sri Lankan Buddhism majorly influenced by Dharmapala's "protestant Buddhism," which later went into the making of the ethnic issue "in terms of a modern Buddhist nationalism," Obeyesekere discusses how Buddhism has "become a religion that has betrayed the heritage of its founder" without "the humanism of Buddhist conscience" (2018, 274). The dismantling of the Buddhist conscience has occurred due to Buddhism becoming a "religion of the head" by losing its previous nature as "a religion of the heart" (Ibid, 272–273). As he argues, it is necessary to understand this process that leads to this "dismantling of the Buddhist conscience" (Ibid, 273) in order to grasp the terrible violence in contemporary Buddhist Sri Lanka (Ibid, 266–274). Nonetheless, it is possible to argue that the purpose of Dharmapala's mission was not to cultivate animosity and vengeance in Sinhala Buddhist mind against the other ethnicities in the country but to save and spread Buddhism in Sri Lanka and the other parts of the world. Yet, his mission becomes problematic only when one explores *how* he tried to materialize his dream.

Dharmapala had taken a militant approach to awaken Sinhala Buddhists to rebuild Sri Lanka as a Sinhala Buddhist nation and liberate Bodhgaya from Hindus (Guruge 1965). His speeches, delivered in Sri Lanka and other parts of the world as a Buddhist missionary and his writings, including the letters to the British Raj, communicate his antagonistic attitude towards the followers of other religions (Guruge 1965; Amunugama 2016). On the other hand, he had also tried persuading Sinhala Buddhist monks to inculcate and strengthen Sinhala national consciousness among Sinhalese, which later influenced the radicalization and mobilization of Sinhala Buddhist monks into Sinhala Buddhist national politics and Sinhala chauvinism (Gombrich and Obeyesekere 1988; Obeyesekere 2018; Tambiah 1992). Thus, the wave rose with Dharmapala's Buddhist revivalist project recharged Sinhala Buddhist mind to revive the legacy of the ancient Sinhala king Dutugemunu written in the Sri Lankan chronicle *Mahavamsa* emphasizing the victory of Sinhala Buddhists over Tamil king, Elara. Here, it is important to quote what *Mahavamsa* writes about how Buddhist *arahants* consoled the Sinhala Buddhist hero King Dutugemunu, who was deeply disturbed, "remembering the destruction of millions (of beings)," and, thus, was unable to be happy over his victory. The conversation between the king and the *arahants* goes like this:

> "We are sent by the brotherhood at Piyangudipa to comfort there, O lord of men."
>
> And thereon the king said again to them: "How shall there be any comfort for me, O venerable sirs, since by me was caused the slaughter of a great host numbering millions?"
>
> "From this deed arises no hindrance in the way to heaven. Only one and a half human beings have been slain here by thee, O lord of men. The one had come unto the (three) refuges, the other had taken on himself the five precepts. Unbelievers and men of evil life were the rest, not more to be esteemed that bests. But as for thee, thou will bring glory to the doctrine of the Buddha in manifold ways; therefore cast away care from thy heart, O ruler of men!"
>
> (David 1912, 106)

The message conveyed by these lines from the chronicle is bizarre, and no one knows how to justify such violent thought said to have been preached by Buddhist *arahants* to the king. Such stupid logic, which cannot be matched with Buddhism, could instigate and facilitate only hate, vengeance, and violence between the communities divided by religion and ethnicity. In this context of the *Mahavamsa*, hate and disgust are simply directed towards Tamils because king Elara is a Tamil king. Here, what makes us worry is not so much what the Sinhala king must have done during the war, over which he already repents, but what Buddhist *arahants* told him *to console* him. However, when Dharmapala revived this ancient legacy of Dutugemunu, and thereby mobilizing Sinhala Buddhists to rebuild Sri Lanka as a Sinhala Buddhist nation, the animosity against Tamils too moved ahead with his movement. It is this desire to continue with the tradition written in *Mahavamsa* by appropriating it as the tradition of the Sinhala Buddhists, which continues to resonate till date, especially when certain Sri Lankan Buddhist monks begin to discourse on why Sinhala Buddhists should refrain from worshipping Hindu gods and why the idols of Hindu gods should be removed from the main shrine at Buddhist temples.[4]

Apart from the violence unleashed by the ethnic conflict between Sinhalese and Tamils, Sri Lanka witnessed another blood bath during the time between the 1970s to the early years of the 1990s, and that is related to the Janatha Vimukthi Peramuna (JVP) insurgency. As Uyangoda (PCD 1, 117) argues, "[T]he JVP insurgency of 1971 and the state's military response to the insurgency was a major landmark in the emergence of violence as a more of political practice, mediation and social control" in Sri Lanka. In 1971, the JVP had operated their first armed revolt against the then Sri Lankan government under Prime Minister Sirimavo Bandaranaike. It, known as "the southern militancy,"[5] revealed the bitter dissatisfaction of the young and the unemployed. It was a well-planned yet failed attempt said to have happened due to the lack of communication (Fernando, April 1971, Colombo Tele.). Hence, it could not seize power. However, the defeat could not bring the death knell to the party and its mission. The second phase of its history, which begins after 1971, is, as Keerawella points out, the so-called "Social Democratic" phase, during which the JVP tried to "enter into the mainstream of parliamentary politics," though "it was not clear whether the JVP genuinely adopted the parliamentary path or whether it was merely a tactical move latter became the strategy and the end itself" (1995, 150). However, since the Jayewardene regime started in 1977 could not address the socio-economic problems, which increased during post-1977 political developments in the country, the JVP was able to emerge "as the main force" capable of challenging the government in a violent manner (Ibid). It managed to gain support from students, unemployed youth, oppressed caste elements, young Buddhist monks, and army deserters (Ibid, 164). JVP's involvement in Sinhala nationalistic activities, which were anti-Tamil, also caused it to become an influential force in the country. Commenting on how the JVP and the LTTE impacted on each other to gain support from the people from South and North, respectively, Keerawella analyzes JVP's inclination to save the pride of the Sinhalese as follows:

> The JVP utilized the psychological impact that the Tamil militancy incurred in the South for its organization and campaign. The challenge to the unity of the Sri Lankan state by demanding a separate state for Tamils was considered a severe blow to the "Sinhala pride." The JVP addressed the wounded national pride and it was prepared and qualified more than any other organization to exploit the situation. Even in 1971, the socialism that the JVP professed was one which was deeply permeated by the nationalistic heritage. In this context, hero worship associated with personality cult gave some credentials to the "Keerti Wijayabahu concept" promoted by the JVP. It was based on the popular perception that a Sinhala hero named Keerti Wijayabahu coming from South would secretly organize and rescue the country from the Tamil invaders.
>
> (Ibid, 161)

JVP's Sinhala nationalistic campaign grew more aggressive and violent in the context of the Indo-Lanka Peace Accord in July 1987. It staged protests openly against the Accord, highlighting India's intention to occupy Sri Lanka. Accordingly, it was a "Patriotic War to liberate the motherland from Indian occupation" and the JVP went on a "war" against the then government led by President J.R. Jayawardene (Ibid, 165). The strength it had gained to mobilize people against the government was so powerful to the extent that people named it the "*Punchi Anduwa*" (little government). In this patriotism, violence was directed against "leading figures and members of the ruling UNP," "leaders and supporters of the left parties who theoretically approved the Peace Accord," "former members of the JVP who were considered to be threat to the JVP leadership", "police officers who were engaged in anti-subversive investigations," and "ordinary people who defied JVP orders" (Ibid, 166). Nevertheless, the government, too, exercised its military power strategically to counter the violence committed by the JVP while annihilating it. Consequently, it deployed a number of "vigilante groups and death-squads" such as "PRAA," "Ukussa," and "Black cats" (Ibid, 171) to suppress the rebellions. Apart from the military tactics, it also used political strategies to silence the JVP.[6]

These two situations during which brutality of hate and vengeance erupted against humanity bring us back to the question posed to Tambiah: "if Buddhism preaches non-violence, why is there so much political violence in Sri Lanka today?" (1992, 1). Now, going by the brief account given above describing two major and recent incidents that highlight violence in post-independent Sri Lanka, one may wonder why I have not commented on the atrocities done by the LTTE. And, that thought alone might be adequate to brand this work as one sympathizing Tamils, non-Buddhists, and the LTTE.

The absence of a detailed account of what the LTTE or other Tamil political parties did to make the country witness such horrific violence does not mean that the work finds any of them innocent. Nor does it mean that the crimes done by the LTTE could be justified. Sri Lanka and the globe could see the violence enacted by the LTTE as a terrorist group to win its goal—Eelam, and those cannot be justified legally, politically, ethnically, linguistically, or in any other manner. On the other hand, being a terrorist group, its survival is undoubtedly on terror and violence against the other. Jayathilaka (2014) provides a detailed account of how LTTE used violence not only against the Sri Lankan state, government, and the Sinhalese but also against the Tamil and some members of the LTTE.

However, this study is not to understand *who* did *what* and *who* did what *first*, if the "what" is about violence. The argument it attempts to place here is, no violence could be justified even if it is done to win love, equality, justice, success, rights, freedom, or peace, either for an individual or for the collective. It also, then, means that it is possible to win love, equality, justice, and freedom even by means of violence or coercion. But, the point to be emphasized here is, what is there to have gained anything for ourselves individually or collectively, if we have obtained it at the cost of the other—be that other is our enemy or our friend, as well as enemy-friend or friend-enemy? This question reminds us of what Gandhi said in *Hind Swaraj* in response to a similar question regarding the presence of the British in India. The question was: "Why should we not obtain our goal, which is good, by any means whatsoever, even by using violence?" (Gandhi 2015, Hind. 105).

Here, the response of Gandhi expresses his *concern*, not so much on *what* the goal is, for it could be anything (in this particular case of India, the goal is freeing India from the British power) but on *how* it is achieved. He, accordingly, underscores the necessity of understanding the fact that *there is* a "connection between the means and the end". Not to believe so is, as he points out, "a great mistake. Through that mistake even men who have been considered religious have committed grievous crimes" (Ibid). In his emphasis on the unavoidable connection between the means and the end, what he tries to make us realize is how different means bring different results, and, thus "to show that fair means alone can produce fair results and that, at least in the majority of cases, if not indeed at all, the force of love and pity in infinitely greater than the force of arms" (Ibid, 13). Considering the "brute force" exercised by the British on India, Gandhi argues how the same force could be used by Indians not only to chase the British away from India but also to suppress the thugs within India. Yet, the point that he attempts to raise here is, there are *other* means other than those of violence that could be invented to obtain the desired goal. And, it is to invent such other means of non-violence that Gandhi turns towards the ancient civilization of India, capable of offering insights on how to *refrain* from committing violence against both self and the other.[7]

Then, Buddhism is one such gift that India could offer to the globe in orienting people towards non-violence. It guides humans to refrain from violence through the practice of compassion to all beings. Every being is capable of such practice if he/she takes a sincere effort to refrain from harming the other while addressing self-desire for happiness, freedom, and so on. Accordingly, it is necessary that every being calling its self into question not only regarding its desires but also, more importantly, on how they fulfil the same. In other words, each action and thought should be self-examined to understand the traces of violence carried within. This effort as an infinite responsibility to non-violence, on the one hand, enables being to liberate itself from the cycle of hate, anger, vengeance, and jealousy simmering within in relation to the other, and, on the other hand, empowers him/her *to self-earn* love, peace, and freedom which cannot be robbed or destroyed by another.

Then, though the question that I have placed above by quoting Tambiah makes us probe into whether Sri Lankan Buddhism has any role to play in aggravating violence in Sri Lanka, on the other hand, it informs the commendable role that Buddhism could play in order to lessen, if not to stop completely, violence happening in Sri Lanka. Hence, the focus of this work is to understand Buddhism as a force of love and compassion that could intervene in addressing the question of violence not necessarily only in Sri Lanka but anywhere in the world by directing individuals and communities to self-righteousness. However, the present-day Buddhism in Sri Lanka is far from becoming such a force of love and compassion since hate, anger, hypocrisy, and arrogance of those who follow it have slowly seeped into it over the years in a way that now it has become a force within which hate and cruelty against the other breeds. Therefore, inventing Buddhism in Sri Lanka as a force of love and compassion remains a challenge in front of us, and the paramount concern of this book is to explore such possibility through literature.

Significance of Literature

This work informs the significance of literature[8] for the deliberation of inventing Buddhism in Sri Lanka as a force of love and compassion. The discussion that highlights the importance of literature to invent religion *otherwise* than the *given* way or *otherwise* than the way it has *already* been *perceived* firstly suggests the significance of understanding literature as a presentation or unfolding of being in its immediacy, which, in Blanchot's word the "crude" (1982, 38), rather than being mere re-presentation of the world *already* out there—an idea from Platonic tradition denigrating literature and its force.[9] If literature is considered only as a mode of representation, there is nothing much to say about literature, because its role is only *to re-present* what is *already* out there in the world. If that is all what it does or what it is capable of doing, it would have some value *only* in some academic space created by language, literature or cultural studies departments in universities, where literary texts are read, interpreted, and understood for producing knowledge *about* languages, cultures, and communities. Those, in turn, would have enabled certain judgements on those languages, cultures, and people. In that sense, a work of literature would have, more or less, played a role of an informant or of a servant who could serve and contribute to the making of Empire(s) including the one(s) in the academic world.[10] Thus, literature would have continued to be a representative servant of colonialism even if the master that it serves must have changed over the years from White to Blacks, including the many shades of grey in between.[11] Hence, the representative character imposed on literature, differently though, both in the context of Plato and, much later, in the context of Western colonialism, undermines what literature is capable of doing, especially without doing nothing—nothing in terms of *action*.[12]

Therefore, this book insists on the force of literature, capable of doing something *more than* and *other than* what it is generally known for, which is the representation of certain reality out there. Before representing, literature *presents*. It is capable of presenting everything, including those which are absent (Blanchot 1995, 300–344). It is able to call (Kamuf 2005) everything into existence by calling out; literature as both call and calling—both noun and the verb. This ability of literature to *call out*, and, consequently, to bring things into existence or presence informs the marvel of language, for literature is language—language as writing.[13]

Accordingly, the idea of literature favoured in this book is the one that is concerned with writing—the act of writing in which literature becomes, as Blanchot argues, the "crude" word of crude being. "The term, 'crude,' derived from Latin, *crudus*, expresses a certain sense of being raw, rough, unprocessed, unprepared, unconditioned, early, naive, primitive, and bloody" (Menike 2020, 248). It could also inversely imply some sense of pureness, which is certainly not the one projected in the binary of pure/impure; rather, in the sense of *as it is*: as it is prior to any processing, correcting, conditioning, taming, reasoning, etc. For Blanchot, the crude word is *prior* to speech. Unlike speech, traditionally considered as the re-presentation of thought and, consequently, the most proximate to thought and being, the crude word is the thought *itself*. It is immediate before becoming the mediator or the negotiator between being and thought. Accordingly, the distance between being and the word as well as being and the thought disappears. They are inextricably united. "Thought is the pure word," says

Blanchot (1982, 40). In "crude or immediate speech, language as language is silent. But beings speak in it" (Ibid).

In speaking in writing—silence, being speaks freely. To speak freely is to say everything without holding back. Therefore, moment of writing, which is *writing moment*, is the moment of freedom in which the writer is "*free* to create a world" of its own (Blanchot 1995, 315). There, things happen differently—differently than how things are ordered and expected to function in the given world of everyday life. But what happens there happens *in* language. It is an invention of language in and through writing. Writing is able to invent[14] everything, including the ones which have not yet been invented. However, this writing moment is crucial since it differs from all other moments which have already passed or which are *to come*—past and future, and this difference of moment is a difference not only marked in and through language but also through being—being *in* writing, also being *as* writing. Accordingly, this difference *in* and *as* language is also the one *in* and *as* being, thinking, and thought. Nevertheless, writing is not only a moment of creation or invention but also is a moment of destruction. It is a force which destroys and creates at the same time. As Blanchot shows, when the writer begins writing,

> his starting point is a certain state of language, a certain form of culture, certain books, and also certain objective elements—ink, paper, printing press. In order to write, he must destroy language in its present form and create it another form, denying books as he forms a book out of what other books are not.
>
> (1995, 316)

Such denial of what *already is* is possible only in literature. Literature denies the everyday world, which is already created in and through denial, negation, or exclusion. The world survives on the borders, which are set to negate or to control what happens at and across borders. It is the world of subjects. However, literature is not interested in what is happening in *this* world. If it does, it is only to express its discomfort or dissatisfaction with what happens in the everyday world. Yet, it does not stop there by becoming a lamentation, complain, or mourning, but goes beyond the world by becoming more than what the world *already is* and what it *could* offer to its being and the beings in it. In that sense, it offers a different world capable of giving something, which the everyday world could not offer, failed to offer, or was hesitant to offer so far. Yet, it is impossible to make this offer(ing) had the world not offered itself with limits. Then, literature happens at the limit—limit of being, language, and the world. Derrida informs this marvel of literature in following terms:

> Experience of Being, nothing less, nothing more, on the edge of metaphysics, literature perhaps stand on the edge of everything, almost beyond everything, including itself. It's the most interesting thing in the world, maybe more interesting than the world, and this is why, if it has no definition, what it heralded and refused under the name of literature cannot be identified with any other discourse.
>
> (Attridge 1992, 47)

Accordingly, by upholding the commendable role played by literature in offering other worlds while informing the possibility of looking at the given world in other different ways, this book offers a discussion on how the writings of Shyam Selvadurai singularly intervene in addressing the question of violence in Sri Lanka.

Shyam Selvadurai's Writings

Shyam Selvadurai is a Sri Lankan-Canadian writer, who writes in English. His oeuvre consists of four novels and two edited books with literary works written by Sri Lankan writers and some other writers from South Asia. However, Shyam's most famous work is his first creation which he published in 1994, *Funny Boy*. The other three novels are *Cinnamon Gardens* (1998), *Swimming in the Monsoon Sea* (2006), and *The Hungry Ghosts* (2013).

These four novels deal with the question of violence in the context of creating identity. Central characters in all his novels face the challenge of being gay in a country like Sri Lanka, where sodomy is a crime. In *Funny Boy* and *Swimming in the Monsoon Sea*, Shyam offers to write about the ignorance of a child, about his sexual inclination and about his desire to be a girl—the other (gender). In the other two novels, *Cinnamon Gardens* and *The Hungry Ghosts*, the two central characters—Balendran and Shivan, respectively—are elders grappling with their sexuality, which makes them outsiders not only to their families, culture, religion, language, and community but also to themselves. The struggle for existence amidst the complexities in which their being(s) unfold(s) in an unexpected and unpredictable manner presents violence against the other as reality of everyday life in the context of being as a subject. Here, Shyam informs the impossibility of defining *what* violence *is* since it could appear or unfold even in the forms of love, care, and friendship.

However, this book is centred on Shyam's latest novel, *The Hungry Ghosts*, since it calls everything in life or everything considered *as* life into question so that one could realize one's own tendency to commit and give in violence, especially while addressing self-desire for love, happiness, freedom, success, and peace. Now, one may ask, why not bring his other works into this discussion, especially when those too are about the same question. In fact, this is one of the questions that came from the scholarly audience during a seminar at the Indian Institute of Advanced Study, Shimla, where I discussed some parts of this book. The question raised by one of the institute's Fellows was, "Your discussion on the question of violence in Sri Lanka is based *only* on one novel by Selvadurai. Why not take his other novels? Also, why not locate this novel with world literature?"

This question, which was and still is very valid, made me say two things in response. The first answer was, "Yes, it does bring other works by Shyam by making some references to them. On the other hand, there are few literary works by Blanchot, Cixous, Shakespeare, Kafka, and Makarand that are taken to discuss the question in writing—violence." My other answer was basically through a reference to what Blanchot had said elsewhere on being in which one being was considered as (a) world. This idea of Blanchot implies something about the number and the value given to them by us, the humans, and the recognition that they have depending on the context they occur. If the recognition thus varies contextually, number *one* is neither the best nor is it the first. At times, it is not a *considerable* number. One of the best examples is how we count the number of dead, injured, or displaced during a war to assess the brutality of war. There, if the number is *more*—more than one, it becomes a matter of concern. If it is otherwise in the sense that if the affected is *one*, it could be ignored since there is a tendency to think that no war could be fought without killing at least one. Such an attitude seems to say, indirectly though, *it is okay to have killed one or two. That is expected.* In that sense, we need more deaths to calculate *how* violent it is. However, this calculation and evaluation with such strange logic of numbers do not make sense to a discourse concerned with ethicalness of violence since it holds life of every being priceless. Marc Crépon (2019) argues, loss of every being as a loss of a place in the Universe—unique and irreplaceable. Therefore, one being is more than being one—singularities.

Similarly, coming back to the number of the texts in question here, how to count the number of texts in a work of literature or is it possible to reduce a literary text to a number *as such*? The answer is determined by how one approaches a text or how one looks at literature. Therefore, my response to the question posed by the concerned scholar was, "For me, one text is full of many world(s) or texts. This is about irreducible singularity." Now, this response might sound defensive and may not be accepted as a valid argument. Yet, this is not an argument but an approach to a work of literature, especially *fiction*. One fiction is about many other fictions, including the one that we are to ourselves. This idea delivers us to the question concerning the relation between literature and philosophy. Franz Kafka, Maurice Blanchot, and Jacques Derrida give a great deal to discuss the affinity between literature and philosophy while problematizing philosophy's stance – a stance held by analytical philosophy regarding literature.[15] Nonetheless, since this question is beyond the scope of this book, we do not need to discuss it here.

Coming back to *The Hungry Ghosts*, unlike Shyam's other novels, it does not highlight the aspect of homosexuality, though it is decisive for the very unfolding of the writing-being. Instead, it appears as the question which problematizes everything else left unquestioned in life – life of both individual and community. Here, the writer calls several communities into question regarding violence: Sri Lankan Sinhala Buddhists, Sri Lankan Tamils, Canadians, and Sri Lankan community of Sinhalese, Tamils, and Muslims in Canada. Each community involves violence to keep the community going. Here, it lets go of the responsibility of caring and protecting life. Most of the story set in Sri Lanka presents the violence that broke out there, especially since 1983. Here, Shyam's take on violence is different from how it is addressed in *Funny Boy,* where he describes the incident of 1983—Black July. The last pages of the novel unfold in the form of a "journal" in which Arjie notes down every incident that he saw, heard, and felt as a child during the riot. But, in *The Hungry Ghosts*, Shyam touches upon all kinds of violence that have been happening in Sri Lanka. Accordingly, he holds everyone responsible for some or other violence happening in society. In that sense, it is not only the LTTE, JVP, and the Sri Lankan state who committed violence against each other, but also civilians who fought with each other just to meet their personal agendas in a time of ethno-political and economic crisis in the country. As far as violence is considered, Shyam does not give importance to knowing *who did what* and *for what reason*, because such knowledge, after a point, cannot help to solve the problem of violence. Rather, it could aggravate the bloody situation, for everyone could produce their own *good* reasons to justify why they have acted in a certain way in certain situations that erupted in history. Hence, his concern is, whatever the case may be, whether it is possible to justify violence *ethically*. In other words, he questions the ethicalness of any violence, even if that violence is committed *to love* or *in the name of love*. He does not differentiate whether this love is for someone or for something.

Emphasizing the necessity of countering such violence as responsibility, Shyam insists on the significance of the Buddhist idea of non-violence through compassion, for it gives equal importance to both ethics and responsibility. In that sense, even the idea of the ghost that unfolds in *The Hungry Ghost* itself is Buddhist that informs, on the one hand, about the one waiting to be freed or redeemed by the other despite and beyond death, and, on the other hand, the possibility of such redemption, if one sincerely holds on to the responsibility to the other despite and beyond death.

One of the significant interventions made by Shyam while writing the urgency of inventing a path leading to non-violence is his suggestion to uphold individual responsibility to non-violence, which is, in his view, not bound by the norms of a community, for the community could enact violence to establish the *order* of non-violence. Therefore, as he argues, the attempt for non-violence is always to begin from the side of the individual, for it could never be attempted collectively, even if everyone in a community shares the desire for non-violence. *The Hungry Ghosts* proposes every being to self-discover this force within, which could empower being to refrain from *ab-use* of power, while trying to address self-desire. Hence, this book strives to understand how Shyam's writing discovers a path for non-violence and how Buddhism influences him in this discovery, which, in turn, plays a commendable role in inventing Buddhism as a force of love and compassion.

Adopting a poststructuralist approach to language and culture as the methodology, the discussion in the book unfolds in four chapters. Accordingly, insisting on the significance of Levinasian philosophy of the other, the first part of the first chapter foregrounds the philosophical question of self-identity in the context of the relationship between self and the other. The second part of the chapter discusses Shyam Selvadurai's thoughts on the impossibility of belonging to any identity *as such*. While providing a sketch of Sri Lanka with its problematic socio-cultural, political, and ethnic situations, especially since the 1970s and its impact on Shyam and his family, it explains how Shyam's idea of "hyphen space" becomes the locus of his being and writings. It is here that the chapter presents Shyam's work, *The Hungry Ghosts*, as the hyphen and the space of hyphen—in-betweenness, openness, and relation.

Focusing on the idea of violence in the context of love, projecting how violence is constitutive to love, the second chapter brings out the impossibility of creating a discourse of absolute non-violence. The discussion exposes the problematics of Sri Lankan Sinhala Buddhist society, which allows certain violence in order to maintain some assumed Sri Lankan Sinhala Buddhist*ness*. In so doing, it projects Shyam's work as a critique of violence in which dominant Sri Lankan Sinhala Buddhist society is called into question with relation to its stand on the other, especially the Tamil, the gay, and women.

The third chapter deals with the question of self-identity in love and responsibility and explores how Shyam's work interrupts the discourse of self-centred love, which demands self-happiness by claiming ownership over the other. Highlighting Shyam's inclination to some Buddhist approach in the attempt of understanding self-love, self-happiness, and self-emancipation, it emphasizes the significance of the Buddhist idea of self-renouncement *to love*. However, here, the chapter engages with the idea of renouncement as the openness to what *to come*, exploring openness as ethical responsibility in the context of self-love. It examines how Shyam invents a unique expression of love and responsibility, which is ethical, radical, and liberating at the same time.

The fourth chapter aims to understand whether the expression of love, therefore that of emancipation invented by Shyam through writing, is necessarily Buddhist. Here, the chapter points out the impossibility of appropriating love, emancipation, ethics, and forgiveness to any religion *as such*, because religion, Buddhism in the present case, itself cannot be thought in terms of *totality*. Similarly, it also informs the impossibility of appropriating or reducing a work of literature to a particular religion *as such* since literature or writing is always outside the given.

Hence, the question worth raising here is whether it is possible to understand religion *as* writing.

Notes

1 The Buddhist idea of ethical responsibility is discussed in detail in some of the following places: five precepts of Buddhism for the laity spelled out in *Sigālovāda Sutta*, the concept of *Atthangika Magga* or noble eightfold path mentioned in *Dhammacakkapavttana Sutta* and *Vibhanga Sutta*, and the concept of *Pāramitā* mentioned in the *Kuddaka Nikāya* in the Pāli canon and in the *Prajñapāramitā sutras* and the *Lotus Sutra* in Mahāyāna Buddhism.

2 Those five precepts are (1) to abstain from killing/murder, (2) to abstain from stealing, (3) to abstain from sensuous misconduct, (4) to abstain from lie and deception, and (5) to abstain from intoxicating drinks and drugs.

3 See S.N. Dube's discussion on "Growth and Ramification of the Early Buddhist Sects and Schools," in *Cross Currents in Early Buddhism* (New Delhi: Manohar Publications, 1980), 37–89. Also see T.N. Madan's ideas on the same in his prologue, "Buddhism, world religion", written to Gananath Obeyesekere's work, *The Buddha in Sri Lanka: Histories and Stories* (Abingdon: Routledge, 2018), x–xlviii.

4 In this regard, see Sinhala Buddhist nationalistic project led by Buddhist monk Gangodawila Soma and his objection regarding Sinhala Buddhists worshiping Hindu gods and other local gods. Apart from the TV and radio programme in which he spoke, please refer to some of his following works written in Sinhala to understand his ideas on the same. Indu Perera, *Misaditu Bindina Handa: Pujya Gangodawila Soma Himi* (Colombo: Dayawansa Jayakody & Company). Gangodawila Soma, *Deshaya Surakina Ran Asipatha* (Colombo: Dayawansa Jayakody & Company). Chamika Munasinghe, *Pujya Gangodawila Soma Himipanange Mage Deshaya Avadi Karana Handa* (Colombo: Dayawansa Jayakody & Company). Stephen C. Berkwitz, "Resisting the Global in Buddhist nationalism: Venerable Soma's Discourse of Decline and Reform," *The Journal of Asian Studies* 67, no. 1 (February 2008): 73–106.

5 Gamini Keerawella attempts to clarify this term in a footnote mentioned in "Political Anatomy of Southern Militancy: The Insurrection of the Janatha Vimukthi Peramuna, 1983–1990," in *Security Dilemma of a Small State: Part Two: Internal Crisis and External Intervention in Sri Lanka* (New Delhi: South Asian Publishers, 1995), 147.

6 For better understanding, please refer to Jayadeva Uyangoda, "Sri Lanka: State of Research on Democracy," *Power conflict Democracy (PCD) Journal*, no. 1 (2017): 97–128, https://jurnal.ugm.ac.id/pcd/article/view/25680/16303; Dayan Jayatilleke, *Sri Lanka's North-South Crisis: Long War, Cold Peace* (Colombo: Vijitha Yapa, 2014).

7 See the detailed discussion offered by Makarand Paranjape on "parampara," "gunas," and "desivad" for critical perspective in this regard. *Debating the 'Post'*

Condition in India: Critical Vernaculars, Unauthorised Modernities, Postcolonial Contentions (Abingdon: Routledge, 2018), 21–98.

8 Please note that in this work, the two terms, "literature" and "writing," are used interchangeably. This use reflects thoughts on literature through writing presented by Maurice Blanchot and Jacques Derrida in their literary and philosophical works.

9 For a better understanding in this regard, please refer to Jacques Derrida, *Of Grammatology*. tr. Gayatri Spivak (Delhi: Motilal Banarsidass, 1994). *Acts of Literature*, ed. Derek Attridge (New York: Routledge, 1992); Maurice Blanchot, *The Space of Literature*, tr. Ann Smock (Lincoln: University of Nebraska Press, 1982). *The Work of Fire*, tr. Charlotte Mandal (California: Stanford University Press, gift); Peggy Kemuf, "Fiction and the Experience of the Other," in *Book of Addresses* (California: Stanford University Press, 2005).

10 Peggy Kamuf offers an engaging discussion in this regard in the essay, "Deconstruction Reading Politics: Democracy's Fiction (Everything, Anything, and Nothing at All)," in *Book of Addresses* (California, Stanford University Press, 2005), 172–188.

11 Makarand R. Paranjape addresses this question while informing the underlying intentions of many academics, even from the so-called Third World, to maintain and uplift the very Eurocentrism, which they seek to problematize in their researches. In a way, he brings to light the hypocrisy *within* the academic domain, whether these spaces are named as Western, Eastern, European, Anglo-American, Subaltern, Asian, Indian or colonial, post-colonial, post-modern, Marxist, and so on. For further knowledge, see Makrand R. Paranjape, *Debating the 'Post' Condition in India: Critical Vernaculars, Unauthorised Modernities, Postcolonial Contentions* (Abingdon: Routledge, 2018), 101–257.

12 Maurice Blanchot's ideas in his discussion on whether "literature is nothing" or "literature is not nothing" are important to understand this idea of non-action or the idea of "passivity" in literature. See Maurice Blanchot, "Literature and the Right to Death" in *The Work of Fire*, tr. Charlotte Mandal (California, Stanford University Press, 1995), 313–319.

13 Here, the idea of language as writing is the one that is discussed by Jacques Derrida in terms of "difference", which is differed presence unavoidable even in the context of speech. However, as he argues, writing has already been identified as that which comes *without*—without the presence of being. It is already fundamental to writing. Therefore, he critically views Plato's hierarchy, which considers speech alone as language, giving the secondary position to writing, and argues how all language is inhabited by writing. For better understanding, see Derrida, Jacques. *Of Grammatology*, tr. Gayatri Spivak (Delhi: Motilal Banarsidass, 1994).

14 The idea of invention emphasized in this work is the one discussed by Jacques Derrida in "Invention of the Other," in *Acts of Literature*, ed. Derek Attridge (New York: Routledge, 1992), 311–343.

15 In this regard, see the discussions brought by Maurice Blanchot and Jacques Derrida in some of their works mentioned below. It is important to note the difficulty in differentiating between Blanchot's philosophical works and his literary works. One cannot be differentiated from the other. All his writings are crucial to this discussion that explores the affinity between literature and philosophy by highlighting how the former influences the later, and vice versa. For a philosophical treatment in this regard, refer to Maurice Blanchot, *Space of Literature*, tr. Ann Smock (Lincoln: University of Nebraska Press, 1982). *Work of Fire*, tr.

Charlotte Mandal (California: Stanford University Press, 1995). *The Book to Come.*, tr. Charlotte Mandal (California: Stanford University Press, 2003). *The Station Hill Blanchot Reader: Fiction & Literary Essays*, ed. George Quasha, tr. Lidiya Davis et al. (Barrytown: Station Hill Press, 1999). *The Blanchot Reader: Maurice Blanchot*, ed. Michael Holland (Oxford: Blackwell, 1995); Jacques Derrida, *Acts of Literature*, ed. Derek Attridge (New York: Routledge, 1992). *Ethics, Institutions, and the Right to Philosophy*, ed. Peter Pericles (Lanham: Rowman & Littlefield, 2002). *Sovereignties in Question: The Poetics of Paul Celan*, ed. Thomas Dutoit (New York: Fordham University Press, 2005).

1

PROMISE TO REMEMBER[1]

> [...] if you love me, if you value the life we have built together, I beg you to tell the truth. The truth that you have, I know now, hidden from me for as long as we've known each other.[2]
>
> (Selvadurai 2013, 336)

How to understand and make sense of these lines quoted from *The Hungry Ghosts* by Shyam Selvadurai?

It places a request, which is a begging: "I beg you to tell the truth." Yet, the begging is not for *this* or *that*, but for truth. The truth at demand is not known to anyone other than *the one* from whom it is requested—Shivan. Shivan is the *only* one capable of telling the truth. Then, it is *his* responsibility.

But, would he tell the truth? *Who* knows? How to assure the truth in telling when the truth is to be told, articulated, or expressed? What if one lies in the disguise of truth? Even worse, what if truth slightly slips by its own and thereby becomes lie in the very act of telling?

Considering these questions, what we could see is, they all point to a problem *of* telling, also *in* telling in which the concern cannot be not only on the one who tells, speaks, or expresses but also on the language that goes into making the same. The problem concerned here is, therefore, a larger one common to all language(s) and all beings speaking in them. It is situated in the already debated yet always debatable philosophical question of language and being.

However, apart from the above questions, the quoted lines lay out another aspect of the request, which is the desire or the quest for truth—*to know* the unknown, an infinite desire.

Now, why such a quest for truth? What does one try to know, especially in a situation like the one quoted above where one is requesting truth from the other?

Hence, Michael's request to Shivan placed by Shyam through his writing broaches too many questions concerning truth. However, the irony is

DOI: 10.4324/9781003045212-2

that we, as humans, who generally do not like problems, especially those of existential kind, due to the suffering caused by them, yearn for truth or yearn *to know* despite the fact that the very desire could deliver us only to further desire and sufferings. In that sense, it implies that, consciously or unconsciously, we are ready to embrace even suffering for the truth by letting go of our comfort, happiness, and also the knowledge or truth that we already have. In any case, ancient Indic traditions communicate this embracing suffering for truth as a practice of life that some people had willingly taken—traditions of renouncement (Obeyesekere 2018, x–xlviii) and self-restraint (Paranjape 2018, 21–81). In a way, it is inappropriate to say that they are *ancient* since they are still at work in different religious societies from the Indian subcontinent. Therefore, these traditions are both ancient and modern at the same time and, thus, not outdated.

However, the request for truth from Michael to Shivan is decisive since it hints at this danger or risk unavoidable to any attempt towards truth. The attempt could either be from the one searching, asking, or requesting truth or could that be from the one trying to reveal, tell, or express truth. Therefore, truth is an event.[3] It could turn everything upside down, destabilizing the *already* established order of things, raising the uncertainty underneath all certainty.

Then, the question before us here is whether one should search for truth by taking a step for truth, which is a step true to one's heart—a true step, a *sincere* one. If yes, to what extent? Could there be limits to such an attempt?

Shyam Selvadurai's *The Hungry Ghosts* presents such step(s) sincerely taken for truth at demand. In presenting, on the one hand, it appears as a response to a call for truth while becoming the danger evoked by the same, on the other hand. In that sense, the appearance of *The Hungry Ghosts* is a response in language through writing that expresses the significance of responding to a call *sincerely*, irrespective of the danger called for by the same gesture of sincerity.

The novel, a work of language as a response, is a way through which one tries to address the other both near and far at the same time. This aspect of the work, first of all, informs the marvel of language by highlighting its unique ability to address anyone or anything despite the distance—the presence and the proximity of being constructed in the binaries of speaker/listener, sender/receiver, addresser/addressee, subject/object, and presence/absence (see Derrida 1994, 27–73). Distance does not matter *to address*, *to call*, *to call out*, and to *summon up* someone or something.[4] A call is able to bridge every distance, and language has always been a call calling out the other. A call is always to some other, for there cannot be a call without the other. Also, every call is always a call for the other.[5] There cannot be a language without the other. It comes with the other (Derrida 1998).

The Hungry Ghosts calls out the other despite and beyond death. It is an infinite conversation with the other, who continues to be present in absence, whose absence becomes the most prominent presence. This gesture of/in language, on the one hand, brings us to another broader philosophical question of being and death. And, the question of death is central to Shyam's work, and the title is already suggestive of that. On the other hand, it is also crucial to writing/literature. There is no literature/writing without death (Blanchot 1992, 1995a). Death gardens literature.

Writing: Death-Writing/Writing-Death

Why Writing? Why Does One Write?

One writes when one is not able to say "I" any longer.[6] This disability is due to the impossibility of identifying oneself as I. However, this is a sudden rupture, split, or break that disrupts the continuity of self-sameness in being, also in language—everyday speech. Speech has been understood as the most authentic and immediate to the being due to its ability to manifest the self-presence of being (Derrida 1994). Jacques Derrida points out this idea, which governs the general notion of language in the present "epoch," to have come down from the Western philosophical tradition of metaphysics—"metaphysics of presence" (Ibid). It has maintained speech alone as language pointing to the "absolute proximity of voice and being and of voice and the meaning of being" (Ibid, 12). Accordingly, speech is the manifestation of self-presence. The idea, the possibility of self-presence in language, informs the ability of the being to identify its own self and to continue to be the same in its being—self-sameness. This ability enables being to realize its being (Self). It is such a realization believed to appear in the *I* language—speech. In that sense, *I* in language, which/who is also the linguistic I subject—the first person and the singular—informs, confirms, and manifests not only the full presence of being as Self but also the power of being determined by the very ability to be its (own) self.

This ability of being, being-able-to-be-Self, communicates being's ability to be self-conscious. Therefore, the linguistic I subject is also the Lacanian conscious subject who makes its entry in the community by identifying its own self as I (Lacan 1980, 148). Being in speech, accordingly, presents its ability to have control over its own being and language, and such control is necessary to become a *subject* of a community or a discourse. As Foucault points out, in a discourse, such submission is *obligatory*, for everyone is "placed under the authority of a syndic," where the individual is under "surveillance," answering to the name and showing the self when asked (1991, 196). Every *subject* is registered in terms of name, age, sex, and so on, and is expected to behave, act, and respond accordingly. Such a mechanism of "panopticon" (Ibid, 200) demands a strong subjection from the subject and it requires continuous self-consciousness, which enables constant self-control and conditioning—"the automatic functioning of power"

(Ibid, 201). Accordingly, the subject, aware of the fact of being *seen*, undertakes the responsibility for the constraints of power and makes them play spontaneously upon the self.

However, this conscious and intentional control of the self is against the other since the presence of the other is considered as the obstacle for the continuity of the self-sameness and the realization of the pure, authentic, and original Self. Hence, existentially, being is in a continuous struggle against the other in order to realize its own self. Pertaining to the question of the relationship between self and the other, the philosophical insights brought by Martin Heidegger, Jean-Paul Sartre, and Emmanuel Levinas are of utmost importance, not only because of how they approach to address the question of being, but also the way in which their philosophies contribute to a discourse on violence in thinking, conceptualizing, and philosophizing what *is* being.

Heidegger and Sartre on Being and Death

Taking a quick look at Heidegger's philosophy of being in his *Being and Time* (1962), Heidegger maintains, the struggle of being against the other is unavoidable till death. Death, being the limit of the relationship of the self with the other, enables being to realize its own being finally—the Self. In the projection of death as the possibility of the self, Heidegger certainly tries to dispel the kind of negativity gone into the general idea or thought *about* death. According to Heidegger, the relationship with the other is not an act of *consciousness* and *intentionality* but a condition unavoidable due to the "thrownness" to the world (Ibid, 174, 219–224). "Dasein" as the "Being-with Others" (Ibid, 159–160), which is an issue for "Dasein" in its very being, should therefore care for its own being amidst "they-self" by reminding itself to return to the "authentic being." It is the kind of responsibility that Heidegger assigns to being (though he does not use the word "responsibility" in his discussion) because the presence of the other makes the being forget about its "authentic being."

Due to this "inauthenticity" in which "Dasein" is dispersed into "they," Dasein's authentic being is "concealed" and "obscured." Consequently, "Dasein" is deviated from discovering the world in its own way. However, Heidegger does not view "Dasein" as the "inauthentic being" negatively; instead, it is considered as that, which enables "Dasein" "to be." To quote it in Heidegger's words,

> In terms of the "they", and as the "they", I am 'given' proximally to 'myself' [mir"selbst"]. Proximally Dasein is "they", and for the most part it remains so. If Dasein discovers the world in its own way [eigens] and brings it close, if it discloses to itself its own

> authentic Being, then this discovery of the 'world' and this disclosure of Dasein are always accomplished as a clearing away of concealments and obscurities, as a breaking up of the disguises with which Dasein bars its own way.
>
> (Ibid, 167)

Dasein's "absorption in" the world as "Being-with Other" through Being-with-one-another, resulting in "thrownness" and "falling," makes him loose and forget its own Self. Therefore, here, "inauthentic" means, "really not"—"Not-Being-its-Self" (Ibid, 220). It "functions as a *positive* possibility of that entity," which, in turn, helps Heidegger to introduce his notions of "care," "anxiety," "resoluteness," "hope," and "returning," communicating some sense of *nostalgia*. It could be easily seen in how he explains the idea of "falling," where *to fall* is described as fall away from something. The "fallen away from" in "the falling," seen as "an alienation" (Ibid, 223), signifies or implicitly refers to some previous location of "Dasein," though Heidegger suggests that "neither must we take the fallenness of Dasein as a 'fall' from a purer and higher 'primal status.' Not only do we lack any experience of this ontically, but ontologically we lack any possibilities or clues for Interpreting it" (Ibid, 220). Therefore, the being that we see proximally "everyday" is "Dasein" as "Being-with Others" and Heidegger defines this "average everydayness" as "Being-in-the-world which is falling and disclosed, thrown and projecting, and for which its own most potentiality-for-Being is an issue, both in its Being alongside the 'world' and in its 'Being-with Others'" (Ibid, 225).

Considering the idea of "fallenness" of being from itself to itself, the phrase, "fallen away from," guides us to locate the direction from where the falling has happened. It is clearly from the Self—*I*, the "authentic being." Now, "falling" is an issue since it hinders the "potentiality-for-Being." Therefore, "falling" results in the dispersal of the Self, and it is the dispersed Self that is encountered as the "subject" to whom the particular dispersion is absorbed (Ibid, 167). This idea of Heidegger—dispersion as unavoidable to "Dasein" as "Being-towards-death"—is similar to the Sartrian view of being as "being-for-itself" to be the "being-in-itself." However, Sartre does not talk about the possibility of *returning* to *Self*. In Sartre, there is no dispersion or absorption of Self into "they-self." Instead, "being-for-itself" for "being-in-itself" is a linear and a forward movement through constant nihilation. It operates to achieve the fullness or totality of being.

However, according to Heidegger, the "falling away from" the "authentic being" obstructs "Dasein" returning to Self—"potentiality-for-being" (Ibid, 183). Such "potentiality" of Dasein, despite the "disguises of everydayness," affirms the possibility of Dasein realizing its authentic being. Then, it is necessary that Dasein remains conscious and makes attempts to realize its authentic being by moving from the "inauthentic." Heidegger, therefore, analyzes Dasein as "the being towards death" and the movement from inauthentic being to authentic being as the journey towards death. Death is, in that sense, no more to be afraid of, sad, and turned away from; instead, it is to be realized by facing it, for it delivers being to its own being—the pure and the authentic being, cut off from the other or "they-self."

According to Heidegger, "the utter loss of Being-in-the-world" (Ibid, 281) is considered as "death," though it is through death that one reaches one's *totality*. "When Dasein reaches its wholeness in death, it simultaneously loses the Being of its 'there'" (Ibid). Death is the totalized "Dasein," though "Dasein" cannot experience its death. It could experience only the death of others. Nevertheless, no one could experience the death of others, "at most we are always just 'there alongside'" (Ibid, 282). Therefore, death is the victorious affirmation of the Self without the other—Being.

In contrast to Heidegger's view, Sartre (1957) projects death as the affirmation of *I* through *negation*. Death alienates self from its life "to the advantage of the Other," because, "to be dead is to be a prey for the living" (Ibid, 543). Sartre's analysis is based on his understanding of living being in which he sees "being-for-itself" as the one constantly active. It is through "being-for-itself" that *I* am able to escape what *I* am for the other by overcoming the other's knowledge "about me." This escape happens not by revealing myself to the other, but

> by revealing to myself by my freely posited ends that I am nothing and that I make myself be what I am; so long as I live, I can give the lie to what others discover in me, by projecting myself already towards other ends and every instance by revealing that my dimension of being-for-myself is incommensurable with my dimension for being-for-others. Thus ceaselessly I escape my outside and ceaselessly I am reapprehended by the Other.
>
> (Ibid, 544)

Then, unlike in Heidegger where living is the affirmation of the impossibility of the Self, in Sartre, living is the negation of the Other. However, both philosophies, differently though, involve negation. In the Sartrian view, negation continues to happen till death in the sense that it becomes the ultimate in the realization of being. Accordingly, death itself is negated, as it is through death, the self is realized as "being-in-itself." But, in Heidegger's, the negation ends with the realization of the Self through death, due to which death is not negated, but affirmed as the affirmation of the Self.

Nonetheless, in Sartre, death is not a possibility that *I* could discover, since it is a "contingent fact which belongs to facticity" and "a certain aspect of being-for-others." Therefore, death becomes the possibility of the *other*, for it permanently alienates "my being," disenabling any escape from the other (Ibid, 545–548). Moreover, it cannot be awaited but could be expected because, "to expect death is not to wait for death" (Ibid). Here, he differentiates between "to wait" and "to expect" as two different acts (Ibid, 535). Accordingly, one "can 'wait for' only a determined event which equally determined processes are in the act of realizing." But, death, despite being inevitable and certain, cannot be determined due to its unpredictable nature. It could be expected since it could come to *me* at any time—"sudden." Hence, death cannot be discussed as something "coming closer" to being. Suddenness is the unique quality of death, which takes being in surprise. "It always, in fact, includes the possibility that we shall die in surprise before the awaited date" (Ibid, 536).

Philosophical stances of Heidegger and Sartre on the being demonstrate the other as the obstacle to be tackled by the self in realizing its being. However, unlike Heidegger, Sartre realizes the other *irresistible*, yet *after* the death of the self. Here, the emphasis on the word "after" is significant, for it points to the possibility of the dead undergoing changes from *outside*. Sartre argues, after death, "nothing more can happen to it inwardly; it is entirely closed; nothing more can be made to enter there; but its meaning does not cease to be modified from the outside" (Ibid, 543). Then, what is upheld in the nihilation of itself *for itself* is nothing but the possibility of the self to *overcome* the other. Accordingly, the transformations of being are not accidental but *consciously* made, since, for Sartre, "there are no accidents in a life." "What happens to me happens through me, and I can neither affect myself with it nor revolt against it nor resign myself to it" (Ibid, 554), because, "each person is an absolute choice of self from the standpoint of a world of knowledges and of techniques which this choice both assumes and illumines" (Ibid, 555). Therefore, though Sartre considers death as the triumph of the other over me, it stands *outside* me and fails to transform me within.

Now, this discussion[7] shows us how both the philosophers foreground the possibility of creating a closure, totality, or empire of the Self in their formulation of being with regard to death, along with a justification of resistance and violence against the other, by pointing to its troublesome and burdensome character. The problematic of such philosophy and philosophizing is, it not only enables, legitimizes, validates, and justifies discourses of exclusion, suppression, domination, exploitation, discrimination, and violence against the other in search of Self-freedom but also necessitates them at both individual and collective levels. So doing, it subscribes to different forms of violence against life unavoidable and inevitable to any discourse of Self-identity.

Levinas: Death and the Other

Criticizing such ontology as a philosophy that calls for violence against the other in promoting Self-freedom, Emmanuel Levinas evokes the necessity of calling such Self-assertive discourse into question. He considers this urgency as ethical exigency, because violence exercised against the other in the pursuit of self-freedom could be problematized only through an enquiry concerning ethics.

Levinasian philosophy claims the impossibility to realize totalized self, for the relationship between self and the other does not come to an end even at death (Levinas 1969). Such unavoidable presence of the other interrupts the "spontaneity of the self" despite its will, and the self is unable to control the other since the other is unknowable and unpredictable. If the other were at the disposal of the self, the latter could have known the former. As Levinas explains, the other is *outside*—stranger. Therefore, the relationship with the other is the one with a stranger in which the self is exposed to strangeness. The exposure is defenceless—vulnerability. Levinas explains this defenceless condition of the self with regard to that of being in the context of death. Death, being "one of the modalities of the relation with the other" for death and other are from the same region, it is unable for the self to terminate its relationship with the other. This infinite relation with the other dismantles the possibility of totalized being. Moreover, in the vulnerable exposure due to the "unforeseeable character" of death (Ibid, 233), as Levinas argues, "I can absolutely not apprehend the moment of death; it is 'out of reach.' My death comes from an instant upon which I can in no way exercise my power" (Ibid, 234). It threatens me from "beyond," and "I am exposed to absolute violence" (Ibid, 233).

Now, the significance of Levinasian thinking of the other is—it not only challenges certain philosophies like that of Heidegger and Sartre, which assert the possibility of self-sameness, but also informs how the concepts of self-consciousness and intentionality serve to strengthen the same discourse. However, the other, always being outside, cannot be seen, grasped, placed, analyzed, categorized, defined, appropriated, and reduced to self-knowledge. This asymmetrical relation is explained by Levinas using the metaphor of "war," placing both the parties, self and the other, face-to-face.

In this confrontation, the self is left only with two options. One is *to surrender*; the other is *to retreat* and *run away*. From the two, the latter is a temporary relief. Here, Levinas discusses how being tries postponing death by saying "not now." The "not now" suggests the being's unpreparedness for death. However, the question here is whether at all being could prepare its being for death through postponing the same? By postponing death, being attempts to take time so that it could prepare well for death. Yet, it can never be well or *adequately* prepared for death due to the ignorance of its arrival—how, when, and where. The unpredictability and the strangeness intrinsic to death disenable all prior preparations made for facing death. Thus, the self is unable to postpone death. Death is the decision of the other, and it comes as its will.

The exposure of the self to the other makes the self-identity tremble. It, however, does not suggest self surrendering the other without any resistance. In Heidegger and Sartre, we saw how the self deliberately attempts to guard its sameness against the other and how consciousness and intentionality become crucial to the deliberation. However, Levinasian other limits such a self-empowering consciousness and intentionality, which, in turn, enables resistance against the other. Such resistance is possible only if the self is *able* to realize the coming of the other. Now, this realization is predetermined by the awareness of the other through seeing, recognizing, and knowing the other as other. It is only then the self could resist the other.

Nevertheless, the problem here is: how could self be conscious and be aware of the other when other is outside—outside vicinity, knowledge, thought, and imagination?

The inability of self to be conscious about the other preempts the possibility of self resisting the coming of the other. *When* it comes, it *comes*; no one could control it. It comes and strikes—event. Maurice Blanchot's *Thomas the Obscure* offers us a literary and philosophical treat about such coming, striking of the other (1999, 51–128). It is the moment of coming that the self is unable to be aware of. The other, somehow, manages to escape the eye that keeps vigil guarding the entry to the domain of the self and sneaks in. And, the self is unaware of such entry of the other. For Levinas, this is how death approaches being:

> It approaches me without being able to be assumed, such that the time separates me from my death dwindles and dwindles without end, involves a sort of last interval which my consciousness cannot traverse, and where a leap will somehow be produced from death to me. The last part of the route will be crossed without me.
>
> (1969, 233)

And, it is "this interference of movements across the distance that separates me from the last moment distinguishes the temporal interval from spatial distance" (Ibid).

Then, Levinas makes two important suggestions through his philosophy of the other. First, the self is in a relationship with the unknowable other. Second, death does not as well as *cannot* end the relationship. Hence, the realization of being in totality as Self remains impossible. Levinas thus offers a different take on death, suggesting the impossibility of defining death as the End of being.

The idea of death as the End of being is problematic. If it is the End of being, everything else connected to that being also should end there in a way that there is nothing left behind, not even memory. In that sense, death becomes the End of all connections. Now, how to agree with this philosophy when we have ancient traditions, which believe in the idea of life after death? How could such philosophy account for the age-old funeral rituals practised and performed by different cultures in the world in the name and the memory of the dead?

Giving a *proper* burial to the dead is an ancient practice in every culture though *that* properness varies from one culture to another. Sophocles' *Cry of Antigone* is a classic example from the literature that reminds us of the necessity of giving a proper burial to the dead. It is the last rite, and it should not be denied, cries and argues Antigone. The burial matters to the life after death, which is not only the one that of the dead but also that of the living—the one who survives the death of the other. Apart from giving a proper burial as the last rites to the dead, different religio-cultural traditions also have some rituals performed *in the memory* of the dead, not just within the specific period of mourning but also after months and years from the death.[8] Those are performed monthly or annually in the name of the dead. These rituals and practices inform and express the impossibility of letting the relationship die along with the dead.

We believe that, in death, one *leaves*. Generally, *leaving* is a euphemistic term that we use in talking or informing someone's death. As an example, we prefer saying *she/he left us* instead of using the verb, *die*: *she/he died* or *she/he is dead*. Here, what we imply is someone leaving *life*. However, it could also have another meaning that proposes some profound thought about death in the sense that death is not about or not *only* about *ending* everything but also about *leaving*—leaving something behind. In each death, there is always something left behind—traces, cinders, remnants, ashes, or memory. The trace is of the dead other (Derrida 1991, 1994, 2001a), and it, in turn, presents the other in absence. Trace is thus both absent presence and presence absent at the same time.

Hence, death does not end the relationship with the other. It instead asserts the impossibility of ending this relationship. The relationship is the only thing that does not die in death; it remains beyond death—infinity. It is this infinite relationship that lies behind all mourning, including all rituals done for the dead (Derrida 1996, 171–192, 2001a). Hence, mourning is very significant and fundamental here. One should mourn over the other. That is how one remembers the other despite and beyond death. The need *to remember* the dead presupposes the forgetfulness of the living. Forgetfulness is the tendency as well as the weakness of memory. Then, *to remember* is to go against this tendency, which is difficult, and it requires some *force* to keep the fading, failing, and dying memory alive *in the name* of the other. Therefore, to remember the other is to take responsibility in the name of the other, in which the other is called, recalled, invoked, and addressed—*I will remember you*. At the same time, it is also a promise at work beneath every relationship (Derrida 2001a; Muffe 2005, 79–90). By morning the other, one tries to keep both promise and responsibility going: on the one hand, responsibility to keep the promise going; on the other hand, promise to take the responsibility going—*to remember*.

The significance of the Levinasian philosophical approach to the question of the relationship between self and the other lies in his insistence on infinite responsibility to the other. To forget or to neglect the presence of the other is to give up on this responsibility. Nevertheless, one could neither be questioned nor could be punished for not taking such responsibility. It cannot be a rule, duty, or responsibility imposable on being like a law or *as* law. It *should not* be. If it *is*, it would be very mechanical. The responsibility under the concern here does not fall under any law; it is outside of the law. Hence, it could be ignored. It is solely up to the being to decide whether to keep it or not. Responsibility without law. Levinas projects it as ethics.

The question of the responsibility to the other is not a question of power or judiciary but one of ethics. It emphasizes the exigency of being questioning its being (self) in the context of its relationship with the other—self-questioning. Self-questioning is prior to the questioning of the other.

However, the idea of the self-questioning under discussion here is different from the one explained by Foucault by referring to the domain of subject where identity plays a crucial role in recognizing being with a community. No one could be a member of a community without recognizing itself with the same. The identity is required in order to be benefitted from it. That is why, as Blanchot writes in *Idle* (1999, 8–33), it was necessary for Akim to identify himself with the community of the house. With such identification, the being takes up self-questioning as a "technique" to check whether its conduct is in compliance with the order of the discourse and alter it accordingly. Foucault elaborates this technique as "care for the self" (Foucault 1997).

Questioning self as an ethical responsibility to the other is different from the former since it prioritizes the other. The other comes first. It is so because, as Levinas (1969) suggests, the presence of the other is a prerequisite to thinking of the self. Accordingly, it is also an approach to self, yet via the other—an indirect way of doing things by beginning from the other, whose infinity is "in-finite" (Derrida 1978, 129).

Such interrogation is not a favourable condition to being since it could shake the very ground on which the being is situated—de-ground. Therefore, being questioning its own being (self) is not as interesting as being questioning another. However, if one dares to take the challenge, then that initiative is a deviation from the concerns of *I* subject—self-identity and self-image. It is a question of, as Peggy Kamuf would say, "what concerns me without concerning me" (2005, 148). In such an act, say, if I may, expedition, being is exposed defenselessly to outside—to what *to come as* and *in* response. Oedipus, the king of ancient Thebes, is a classic example that exhibits the danger of defenceless exposure (Sophocles 1967, 25–68), where being remains unconditionally open to what *to come*—future.[9] However, the domain of the subject does not entertain or encourage such unconditional openness in being because, let alone the subject, the very idea of the subject itself legitimizes a presupposed closure in being. Hence, the sincere effort of questioning the self could be attempted *only if* being steps outside the subject.

But, How to Step Outside the ***Subject***? Is It Possible?

There is no given method or way to step outside. It cannot be given but to be invented. It is here, language as writing becomes significant. Writing is able to invent (Derrida 2007, 1–47). When I say, language as writing, it does not refer to alphabetic writing, a system of writing, or systematic writing. Instead, it emphasizes the idea of language as writing proposed by Derrida (1973, 1994) and Blanchot (1995a, 1999, 471–486) in their respective approaches to understanding being. Accordingly, writing invents language. By inventing language, it invents everything—literature (Blanchot 1995a, 300–344).

To write means to move from *I subject* and speech. It is a shift from the conditioned being to unconditioned being, conditioned speech to the unconditioned word. According to Blanchot, unconditioned being and word are those prior to subject and speech. He terms them as "the crude" (1982, 39–40). The crude word, being the one *prior* to speech (since speech is considered as re-presentation of thought), is thought. Therefore, it is no more the mediator or the vehicle of thought but the *immediate*. Thus, Blanchot undoes the classical distance between word and thought. "Thought is the pure word" (1982, 39). However, in this crude word, the being speaks in *silence*: "language as language is silent. But beings speak in it" (Ibid), says Blanchot.

In his idea of crudeness and immediacy in writing, Blanchot differentiates writing from the common language of communication. Immediate language is a relation with the immediate world. However, the immediacy communicated to us via common language is actually a "veiled" distance because of the force within language, capable of hiding the moment. Language exercises this force in communication. It communicates the illusion of immediacy while giving us only the habitual, and thus makes us believe that the immediate is familiar (Ibid, 40–41).

Nevertheless, Blanchot's idea of illusion and the habitual in the context of everyday being and everyday language is not similar to the idea of concealment explained by Heidegger (1962), which suggests being of the everyday as the one far from Real—"inauthentic being." The Real is the Self, and it is to be deciphered in the "inauthentic being" lost in idle chatter of everydayness. Hence, he insists, being should end the relationship with the "they-self" so that it could be The Real—the absolute, authentic, and the original I—absolute closure. Contrastingly, Blanchot proposes the opposite by emphasizing the impossibility of finding being in absolute interiority. He maintains being and language as *outside*—outside the given world, given subject, given language. Therefore, it is necessary that the self opens up to *outside*.

Writing opens up being to outside/other by undoing the self-closure. Being is moved from the domain of I subject and delivered to some *other* domain, where both being and language unfold as other: other being(s) and other language(s). Being speaks in (an)other language. *I* as some other in other name(s). Writing enables and facilitates this "ruse" to express. Opting to respond to a question by writing a letter to Nayan in *Body Offering* (2013), Paranjape places the urgency of writing since it is enabling. According to him, it not only enables one's response, answer, speech, or expression but also could make it sincere, since it facilitates a passage for being to move from its subjective position to another—"third person" (2013, 108). The movement, shift, slip, or displacement is necessary if to express sincerely. Sincerity matters *to express sincerely* (Menike 2020).

Since the movement is from conscious I subject to other, writing could also be seen as the unfolding of the unconscious, which, according to Freud, is the repository of repressed desire. Now, the problem with Freudian and Lacanian psychoanalysis is, they attempt to read *into* this desire in order to find out what *is* actually repressed *in* the desire—pathology. Going another step ahead, Lacan reduces this desire to be the infantile sexual desire for the mother's body. So doing, they not only suggest the presence of some secret *already there* in terms of "there is" but also the possibility of detecting it and decoding it with the help of applying methods so that the meaning hidden could finally be deciphered.[10]

Writing is a desire *to* express—to express, to say, to present that could not be said or spoken. In that sense, it is certainly related to some repressed desire, not necessarily sexual though (Deleuze and Guattari 1987). It could be pathological yet cannot be medically intervened—incurable. If writing is about expressing, there is nothing *to be* deciphered in writing other than writing, both verb and noun or act and the action. The one in writing, the writer, does not intend to hide because, the impulsion to write, desire uncontrollable, is determined by the impossibility of hiding, avoiding, neglecting, or suppressing the desire to be open and sincere. If there is such an intention to hide, *why* write?

Writing exposes, expresses, and liberates. It does not subscribe to the utilitarian notion of language that highlights its instrumental aspect. To project language as an instrument is to maintain the Platonic hierarchy of thought and language. Contrastingly, the idea of writing—literature—under discussion here does not identify such order, differentiating thought from language. Instead, it insists on the inseparability of one from the other—thought from language, being from language. Therefore, if writing is a repressed desire unfolding, it is desire itself, language itself, thought itself, the expression itself, and being itself—"the crude".

Being opens in language, in literature. Literature is opening in language—eruption, rupture, crack, cut, wound, split, fissure. In this opening, it opens up to the outside while interrupting the ongoing language. Therefore,

Derrida terms writing as "violent opening" (1994, 140) in both language and being.

Shyam Selvadurai

Some problems in life cannot be solved by providing *one* good answer. Every good answer is, on the other hand, the least bad and, thus, fails to be the ultimate, which could eliminate the possibilities of re-occurring the same problem. Such problems keep us engaged in an infinite conversation with our selves; make us question ourselves regarding our previous solutions pointing at our partialities, inclinations, and positions. Meanwhile, we also realize, most of the present problems are aftermaths of our response to some other situation, condition, or problem. It is those responses, once most wise and well-thought, later become most stupid and troublesome. But, what could we do about it? Is it our fault that we could not foresee the future possibilities of one becoming another?

If we could see how, at times, we get ourselves trapped by our own responses, if we could calculate all future possibilities, including impossibility enabled by those, if our knowledge could tell us what *to come* in response to a response, we would not have responded the way we did. We would have responded differently. Yet, who knows? Who could tell which response is better (than another) until one is made? Here, we always run the risk of being guilty due to ignorance.

No one could be aware of the future *to come*—ignorance. There is ignorance behind every response, step, or solution. Every step, no matter how educated we are, is thus a step of ignorance. No knowledge could be adequate to eradicate it. There is always *outside*. However, this is not to say, one should not respond. One anyway responds. The act *cannot* be avoided all together. At the most, as Derrida (1995b) would say, in responding, one could choose to be silent. In fact, responding is probably the only thing that one *cannot* avoid. One cannot *not* respond—responsibility. In such a responsibility, one is defencelessly open to the other/outside—future. Now, it is such unconditional and defenceless exposure in response and responsibility that makes literature, writing, fascinating—fascinating philosophy.

In writing, one takes up this dangerous responsibility. It certainly requires courage. Writing is a response to a call of the other/outside (Blanchot and Foucault 1987, 9–58). This response remains open to the other. On the other hand, writing is also a call. It calls out the other. Now, Shyam Selvadurai's *The Hungry Ghost* (2013), both title and the work, is suggestive of this vulnerability of the being bound to the other in a response—responsibility, which, in turn, enables being to overcome its own being.

The chapter began with some lines from the novel, which place a request for truth. Shivan, the protagonist, is before this request. He should respond to it. Yet, it is solely up to him *how* to respond. He has the ability *to respond*. It enables him not only to reveal the truth but also to hide the truth by saying something else in the place of truth; consequently, *that* would take the place *of* truth in taking place as truth. However, the request too is not simple. It comes with the condition that emphasizes the necessity of truth *only if* one loves the other (Nalika 2019).

Michael says, "Shivan, *if* you love me, *if* you value the life we have built together, I beg you to tell me the truth" (Ibid, 336, italics added).

Then, the request is tricky. Michael does not simply ask something that Shivan *could* give easily, nor does he ask something that he *cannot* give. It is not about giving or not giving but giving *only if* one *wants* to give (Derrida 1995a). In such giving, one cannot give to impress the other, because the one, who gives, does not know whether the other at the receiving end would be impressed by what is given. This choice does not belong to the one who *gives*. At the most, the giver could only *hope*.

Then, the request has brought him to some edgy situation.

He says, "I was at the end of my rope, and there was nowhere to go except to the truth or its alternative, the end of our relationship" (Selvadurai 2013, 336).

For him, the alternative is harsher than the truth at demand. He is unable to end the relationship with Michael. Hence, he should surrender himself to *this* truth—the inability to end the relationship, and reveal the truth in question. Now, the aporetic situation sprung before Shivan is also the one before the writer Shyam. He too is summoned by a call to write—irresistible desire to express the suppressed, the silenced, or the unsaid. If he resists this desire, he resists truth—the other. Truth, like the other, is unavoidable. It comes, *anyway*—force. Hence, one could only surrender.

In writing, the writer surrenders to the force of writing desire—call to write. But, in writing, writing too surrenders to the writing force emanating from writer—response. One is capitulated by the other. Writing could happen only in such bidirectional relations between one and the other, where one is open to the other like in love, possible only in opening the barriers held against (an)other being. It is such openness that is at demand before the writer, as well as before the character that appears in writing, Shivan.

Shyam should write speaking in (an)other name; Shivan should speak in love for the other. Shivan's expression, speaking, or voice is enabled by Shyam in and through writing. Shyam invents Shivan in writing. Writing invents not only Shivan but also being and language—Shyam and the work. Nonetheless, in this invention, it is difficult to find out who invents whom: Shivan through Shyam or Shyam through Shivan. The clarity of the origin is undecidable, for the invention is bidirectional. Therefore, the invented being in writing is neither Shyam nor Shivan in the absolute sense. It is one *through* the other. Writing blurs the boundary between one and the other in such a way that it disenables the recognition, differentiating one from the other—identity. Writing thus offers one and the other at the same time—Shyam-Shivan and Shivan-Shyam—informing how self-identity trembles at the border of writing.

Shyam Amidst the Question of Identity

Shyam Selvadurai was born in Sri Lanka and lived there for 18 years bearing Sri Lankan nationality. Sri Lanka is thus his birth right—legal connection.

But is his Sri Lankan connection only a legal one? Could we reduce it to be *only* that?

If it is the only way he is connected to Sri Lanka, it is no more valid as he has migrated to Canada at the age of 19 years.

In any case, how far could law succeed in validating or de-validating human connections or relations? Sometimes, what happens is, relationships outlaw the law in a way that law has to invent new laws in the name of justice (Derrida 2002a, 230–298).

However, for Shyam, Sri Lanka is more than and beyond legal right. It is a gift of love from his mother on his birthday, connecting one with the other emotionally. Such connections, which are Sri Lankan, cannot be cancelled by migration. They follow him to Canada, crossing miles across the ocean and continents. Those heart-felt relations become crucial to his being since they continue delivering him to the question of self-recognition, *who* am *I?*—identity. This confrontation never comes to an end, for Shyam's being is always *to unfold—infinity.*

Conflict

Nevertheless, considering Shyam's Sri Lankan connections, it is important to contextualize the country, Sri Lanka, which unfolded during his time—the post-independent Sri Lanka.

The recently ended ethnic war between Sinhalese and Tamils is a widely known issue about the post-independent Sri Lanka. The enmity between majority Sinhalese and minority Tamils has a long history, and the *Mahavamsa* provides a descriptive analysis on this matter. As the chronicle shows, it is during the time of Sinhala Buddhist king, Dutugemunu that the northern part of the country was redeemed from the clutches of the Dravidian king, Elara (David 1912). However, British colonial policies before 1948 and some political steps initiated by Sinhala Buddhist political leaders in post-independent Sri Lanka rekindled the hatred between the two ethnicities distancing them from each other for many years to come. At the same time, Anagarika Dharmapala, the great Sinhala Buddhist reformer who had begun his mission of reawakening Sinhala Buddhist Nationalist discourse not only to resist British imperialism but also to mock at Hindus and Muslims in the country "who are 'superstitious,' 'idolatrous,'\ 'pagan,' and given to crude doctrines," galvanized Sinhala Buddhists with the legacy of the hero King Dutugemunu (Guruge 1965; Amunugama 2016). His message to the young men of Ceylon was, "Enter into the realms of our King Dutugemunu in spirit and try to identify yourself with the thoughts of the great king who rescued Buddhism and our nationalism from oblivion" (Guruge 1965). Commenting on how Dharmapala's Sinhala Buddhist identity affirmation continued to influence Sinhala Buddhists not only in the pre-independent Sinhala Buddhist society in the early twentieth century to hold up the "glories of the Sinhala past as an ideal worth resurrecting" but also in mobilizing Buddhist monks and Buddhist lay people for a Sinhala Buddhist nationalism, Obeysekere (2018) informs the role played by "village intelligentsia" of which monks were a part in the formation of the "leadership in Sinhala villages", which in turn

> mobilized the village vote for the first time in 1956 and brought the popular Prime Minister Bandaranaike into power. Bandaranaike, though himself unaware of it, reaped the heritage of Dharmapala. It was the children of this stratum or their children's children that led the 1971 youth insurrection in Sri Lanka. The ascetic dedication, rigid Puritanism and organizational skills of the 1971 rebels, and their narrow chauvinistic adaptation of Marxism, reflect at least partially the now waning influence of Angarika Dharmapala.
>
> (Ibid, 297)

Amidst such racial and religious prejudices in which Sinhala leaders continued to turn a blind eye to the sufferings of Tamils, some Tamil groups, who stood for the liberation of the Tamil, sought independence from Sinhalese taking a path of violence. For them, the solution for the unrest of Tamils in Sri Lanka was separatism (Jayathilake 2014). They dreamt of a country of their own, which could give them freedom and dignity—the Tamil Eelam. Thus, the animosity between the two ethnicities escalated over the years to the extent that it culminated in 1983 riots—Black July erupted with the news of the Liberation of Tamil Eelam (LTTE) murdering 13 soldiers from the Sri Lankan army in Jaffna. Colombo was the city most beaten by the flames of anger, hate, vengeance, and cruelty (Hoole 2001). Though this was not the first anti-Tamil riot in post-independent Sri Lanka, this particular one is crucial since its fire continued for more than two decades in a massive war despite all cease-fire attempts bargained and negotiated between the Sri Lankan state and the LTTE with the intervention of other countries and international organizations. Consequently, both sides went on killing people with a justification of their own.

Nonetheless, apart from the ethnic issue, there was another tension going on in then Sri Lanka, and it was created by the radical leftist movement led by Janatha Vimukthi Peramuna (JVP). JVP was more of a Sinhala party. Its demands were different from those of the LTTE, though both had expected liberation as the ultimate goal. However, since the government did not entertain the demands made by the JVP, it became aggressive and adopted violent means to threaten the government in order to meet their demands. Then government ruled by the United National Party (UNP), a right wing political party in Sri Lanka, too was very determined to eliminate the JVP by using all possible means of violence. Consequently, both parties were involved in numerous incidents such as abductions, killings, raping women, ransacking properties, burning people alive, silencing intellectuals, and various other kinds of possibilities. Yet, none of them took the responsibility of committing any such violence. Without having anyone to shoulder, the responsibility, thus, oscillated between the two amidst the weeping relatives of the dead, the wounded and the disappeared. They did not care for anyone else other than themselves, and thus fed on others' lives. Accordingly, the country during the 80s and the 90s witnessed bodies burning at junctions, mutilated ones floating on rivers, and pieces of clothes hanging from trees, electric poles or railings of bridges. Thus, violence had unfolded in unimaginable forms making the island dark, gloomy, and panic-struck. Then, Sri Lanka that Shyam had lived in was one during the problematic time of the 70s to the early 90s.

Shyam Selvadurai: the Hyphen

In Sri Lanka, the name, Shyam Selvadurai, is easily recognized as a Tamil name. It communicates certain Tamilness attached to him though no one knows what that Tamil*ness* is. It is assertive of his Tamilness rather than of his Sri Lankanness (if such Tamil*ness* or Sri Lankan*ness* actually exists). Since Tamils being the old enemy in the Sinhala Buddhist consciousness reflected in the state machinery, any Tamil was a potential tiger by default if not one *already*. Hence, the identity as a Tamil in Sri Lanka has been dangerous.

But is it the only identity that a Tamil could have? What if there are exceptions?

Shyam's family is a mixture of both races. His father is Tamil, and his mother is Sinhalese (2004, 3). He is, therefore, a confluence of these two races, two religions, two cultures, two languages, two genders, and two people. He *is* confluence, as well as the *other* of the two. He is *(an)other* in terms of person, race, language, religion, culture, and gender—*third* person and *third* space beyond the two. In such a context, his Tamil*ness* carries certain Sinhala*ness*, and vice versa.[11] It is impossible to separate one from the other because one does not come without enabling the coming of the other. This situation informs the impossibility of pure identity in terms of race, culture, religion, language, and community. Nevertheless, what we have discussed so far is related to Shyam's ethnic identity. But, there is one more dimension, which is significant in the context of Shyam and his writings. That is his sexuality.

Shyam is gay BUT in Sri Lanka. The combination—being gay and being Sri Lankan—does not go well together. It cannot be a combination possible in Sri Lanka, but outside. Outside Sri Lanka, it is a possibility or even a right that a Sri Lankan might have (Selvadurai 1998). Sodomy, an aspect of homosexuality, is a crime in Sri Lanka.[12] Its law does not accept or approve gay relationships. Yet, if there is any such, he is an outlaw. However, despite this law and the order of the state, also that of the society, Shyam happens to be both—Sri Lankan and gay.

Now, how to live this contrary, especially when it is prohibited? Commenting on how he felt about himself when he realized his sexual orientation, Shyam says:

> On a personal level, I was also beginning to come to terms with being gay, beginning to live out another very important part of my identity. It was very clear to me that the pure sense of being Sri Lankan was based on rigid heterosexual and gender roles. Where did someone like me belong then? By being gay, was I no longer Sri Lankan? And if that was not the case, what did it mean to be both Sri Lankan and gay; how to live out this combination of identities.
> (Selvadurai 2004, 4)

Migration from Sri Lanka to Canada

The traumatic experience of the 1983 riots in Sri Lanka compels Shyam and his family to migrate to Canada. This migration makes him a Canadian by law.

Yet, is it actually possible for him to be a Canadian just because of the grant of Canadian citizenship?

He *cannot.*

There are new challenges to face, and he should make attempts to overcome them. On the other hand, new challenges are even tougher than the old ones. When he was in Sri Lanka, he had to face only those to do with Sri Lanka. Now, life in Canada is about both Canada and Sri Lanka—two countries from two different continents loaded with their own problems. His problems are now those he faces as a Sri Lankan *in* Canada, as well as a Sri Lankan *and* a Canadian—complex situation of having to live at two different places at the same time.[13] He attempts to verbalize this inexplicable condition which dis-enabled him, on the one hand, leaving Sri Lanka *completely* and, on the other hand, reaching Canada *finally*.

> It was the arrival in Canada that shook it. Here, for the first time, I found myself forced, like almost all new immigrants, to ask myself these questions about who I was: What did it mean to be Sri Lankan? What aspects of my culture made me Sri Lankan, what aspects didn't? What was the essence of Sri Lankanness?
>
> (Selvadurai 2004, 3).

He has stepped out from Sri Lanka to reach Canada. But has he been successful in his attempt?

Stepping out aimlessly is different from the one with some aimed destination. The former is risky, as one is absolutely exposed to the unknown even if it does not require planning. The second needs some planning and calculations to reach the destination.

But, do such planned attempts always succeed? In spite of all plans, what if the target is missed due to some unexpected unfolding of an event? Shyam writes about such an incident in *Funny Boy*, where Arjie fails at the last leg of the game, "bride-bride" due to the unexpected appearance of Kanti aunty (1994, 12–13). Such missing outs cause frustration not because of *not reaching where one wanted to* but being *almost* there yet not *exactly*. There is a *minute* difference between the two: between being *exactly* there and being *almost* there. As Cixous says, this difference could be similar to the size of a pencil stroke or strand of hair (2005, 43–62). Yet, it *matters*. Like any diasporic, Shyam, too, is in this condition of despair and frustration. He had moved out from Sri Lanka with the purpose of reaching Canada; he has reached Canada too. However, there is someone in him, who is *yet* to leave Sri Lanka, and thus not made to Canada. Hence, he could neither be fully Canadian nor could he be fully Sri Lankan—*in-between*. Shyam prefers naming this in-between space as "hyphen." It is a "marvellous open space,", as he says, "in which the two parts of my identity jostle and rub up against each other like tectonic plates, pushing upwards the eruption that is my work. It is from this space between that the novel come" (2004, 1–2).

Shyam is the hyphen—link, opening, and space.

Hyphen is a non-phonetic element of language, and it could occur only in writing. Being a graphic intervention, like "a" in *differance* (Derrida 1973, 129–160), it could neither be pronounced nor could it be heard—silence. Hence, Shyam speaks in silence —writing.

What does he write?

Shyam writes what could not be said. The unspoken is urging to speak, and he is unable to suppress it any longer. He cannot help this inability. Further postponement is impossible. He should speak *now*—urgency. This urgency is also like some emergency, where one does not have time *to think* and calculate the response and its aftermath (Derrida 2002b, 295–314). One should decide quickly without having any prior knowledge about the future and be ready with a "yes" *to come*. If it is thus dangerous, one should not have postponed saying what needs to be said. He could have told it before and avoided the accidents, which tend to occur when spoken in a rush during an emergency. It could have been said when there was enough time *to speak* and when there was time *to take*.

But, isn't it what he, Shyam-Shivan, has been actually doing so far—taking time *to speak*?

Shyam writes the writing condition: the condition in which one writes and the condition that writing leaves *in* writing.

Writing takes time to speak.

All this while, he has tried to speak, to say, to express which could not be expressed so far. Shyam writes how this need had kept him (Shivan) occupied with figuring out how to say, when to say, and where to say. He had wanted to manage all these to speak and to express. Once he manages to bring all these together, he had thought, it would be the perfect time to speak. Then, he has been taking all this time of his relationship with the other to find out the proper time. While waiting for a proper or a better time, unconsciously though, he has passed all the time that he had. Meanwhile, time, being so independent—other, keeps coming to pass without offering *the* time for which one waited (Blanchot 1997). Each writing is pressed and pushed by such desire to be perfect in writing, expressing, or saying. It is a desire for perfection. So long as the being is driven by such desire for perfection in language, sincere writing, speaking, and expressing are impossible. The effort is suspended by the concern for the self-image constantly at work with the fear of losing it. It is possible to lose the concerned image since it is the condition of the image. One fears this condition and tries to care for the same as much as possible so that the image is intact. That is why careful speech could always be questioned regarding its genuineness or sincerity.

However, as discussed above, writing, the expression sincere, could come only when the concern for self-image is overcome by the impulsion to express sincerely, even if that would amount to expressing some defect, weakness, unacceptability, insincerity, dishonesty, or imperfection of the one in the expression. In such impulsion, the concern is to express without searching for perfection, clarity, and preciseness. It is the urgency of writing, the act that cannot be postponed further. It is necessary to speak *now* and *here*—writing.

Insisting on the urgency of writing, Blanchot's *Death Sentence* (1999, 129–187) informs about some hurriedness that could come even after nine years. Blanchot needs to express something that had occurred to him nine years ago. He has already made attempts to write, but failed. It takes nine years for him to feel the irresistible urgency of writing. However, it is not a problem only about time, but also about language. He says, "there are ten words to say. For nine years I have held against them" (Ibid, 131). Then, it is a matter of "ten words" that goes for nine years. Language holds him back in expressing the truth that he knows. It fails him, and he fails in language. Also, it fails truth, and truth fails in it, since "words are frailer and more cunning" (Ibid). Yet, he *cannot* give up on this effort to tell the truth. If he gives up, he betrays himself by hiding the truth. Betrayal is unavoidable in language (Nalika 2019, 8). He has to make the choice of *either/or*. If he chooses to not express, it would be a deliberate attempt of silencing some truth and knowledge that enable certain future—future of thinking, thought, language, expression, and desire. On the other hand, if he chooses to express, he would be subjected to the betrayal of language, delivering him to criticisms, misunderstandings, misinterpretations, as well as, to a death sentence,[14] yet, it would assure that there would be a future, whether good or bad. Blanchot finally decides to go with the latter by writing *Death Sentence* "freely" because, he says, "this story concerns no one but myself" (Ibid).

Similarly, Shyam, too, is compelled to speak freely notwithstanding such betrayal—writing. So doing, he betrays himself as if self-betrayal is a prerequisite to express freely in which not only the expression but also being in the expression unfolds as freedom.

Here, one may ask, what is the point of such freedom if it comes at the cost of self; if it comes in *my* absence? Then, would it still be *mine*? Does that freedom belong to *me*?

Freedom does not belong to self but to the other. The absence of self-presence preempts the possibility of self-belonging. This idea of freedom resonates with the Buddhist idea of *nirvana* (emancipation) that could be attempted only by attempting to free the self from the desire for self-belonging. In fact, the idea of *nirvana* is prominent in Shyam's *The Hungry Ghosts*. Therefore, one tends to feel the idea of freedom that appears in Shyam's writing is Buddhist. But, is it actually so? We have been discussing writing, which is both free and freedom. Writing frees the self. So doing, it delivers being into enormous freedom. Therefore, writing *is* freedom. On the other hand, it is also *about* freedom. *The Hungry Ghosts* is about freedom while being freedom itself. Shyam writes about freedom with the help of Shivan's familiarity with some Buddhist *Jataka* stories. Those *Jataka* stories narrate freedom from the Buddhist point of view. Accordingly, the idea of freedom in the novel is a Buddhist idea of freedom.

But, the question here is, whether freedom that unfolds *in* writing could also be seen as Buddhist?

Hence, withholding this question to be discussed in the later chapters, let's see how Shyam-Shivan responds to the call of *The Hungry Ghosts*.

The Hungry Ghosts

Call of *The Hungry Ghosts* is disturbing as it is interruptive and interrogative; on the other hand, it is consolatory since it is inventive. It poses some grave questions *of* violence, love, hospitality, forgiveness, truth, Buddhism, freedom, and democracy. But, those questions do not appear in the form of a question starting with "what"[15] as in "what is violence?", "what is love?", "what is forgiveness?", and so on. Also, they are not directed to anyone particularly. They are open questions. Nevertheless, having not been directed to anyone particular, they are directed to everyone (Blanchot 1999, 471–486) in the sense that they concern everyone; so, everyone could respond to them in their own singularity. Everyone would have their own opinion regarding these matters. It is possible one finds such questioning useless since it does not aim to find an answer. It does not mean that there are no answers to such questions. Rather, there could be answers but less assuring—uncertainty. Literature/writing in its openness subscribes to this uncertainty as only assurance or certainty on which it could vouch in existence. Therefore, the writers do not write to find answers. Writing does not provide answers. It cannot. A writer writes because there is no answer other than writing—passivity. Commenting on those who write, Blanchot says, "people who are in favor of action reject literature, which does not act, and those in search of passion become writers so as not to act" (Blanchot 1995a, 313).

The Hungry Ghosts (2013) unfolds as Shivan's life unfolds in relation and response to his relationship with others. He is disturbed due to these relationships; yet, not able to undo any of them. That causes dismay. He would not have realized the impossibility of undoing had he not tried to undo. There cannot be failures without attempts; later confirms the former. Since childhood, he has been very busy with this task of undoing the things done by him, as well as by others (Ibid, 23–42). Some temporary reliefs made him even believe that he was successful. They could ease out the tension for some days, months, or years, compelling him to pursue a permanent one that could come only when *everything* is settled. Hence, he took different steps to settle down things with others, starting from his own family members to his two friends with whom he had fallen in love. He wanted to move ahead with his steps.

In fact, he has been doing *only* that since he stepped into his grandmother's house along with his mother and sister, Renu (Ibid). The step of moving from Sri Lanka to Canada itself is his initiative desiring a life full of freedom. He had planned everything—from cycling to the Canadian High Commission on Gregory's Road, misleading the guard with his lies to get the form for "fast-track immigration" to Canada, persuading his mother and the sister to agree with his decision, meeting all the necessities to fly Canada while hiding things from his grandmother and to finally taking the flight to Canada with his mother and the sister—in pursuit of "freedom" (Ibid, 71).

"But think of the life we could have there, Amma. Renu and I could go to a foreign university. Think," I held her gaze, "of the *freedom for me*" (Ibid, 68, italics added).

Life in Canada is also about this freedom and its happiness. Desiring freedom and happiness is not a problem. It is what everyone desires. It becomes problematic, nonetheless, depending on *how* it is desired; *how* one approaches to address it. According to Shivan, freedom could be imagined only if one understands "how" one might "escape" (Ibid, 55)—freedom through escape. So, he, especially since the age of 17 years, tries escaping every demanding situation, people, and place. Migration to Canada is one such escape made imagining the freedom and happiness that the new place could offer to him. He is moved by the imagination of life with freedom.

But, isn't the goal itself an imagination?

One might be able to escape certain situations, people, and places. Yet, there are certain things in life, like the past, which do not offer such an option. One cannot escape the past because, "like a leopard stalking its prey through tall grass, a man's past life pursues him, waiting for the right moment to pounce" (Ibid, 319), Shivan, too, is vulnerably exposed to his past. It pays him sudden visits, which are, for him, of *The Hungry Ghosts*. It comes behind like how *karma* does. Past never disappears absolutely. It leaves a trace. Trace does not disappear. It appears and affirms the impossibility of absolute disappearance. One should not forget the presence of the trace presenting presence absence. Therefore, one should look back while moving ahead; it is only then one could realize the appearance of the disappearance. Shivan is reminded of this response, responsibility, by the story of King Nandaka (Ibid, 25) narrated to him by his grandmother.

It is a story about the disappearance of a road that the king and his troops had travelled after a victorious war.

> He reaches a crossroads, and seeing that one of the avenues is smoothly paved and shaded with trees, he takes it, not realizing it lead to the haunt of peréthayas. Soon his men grow fearful, as an odour of rotting flesh blooms around them and wailing shimmers the air. Looking back, they see that the road they travelled has disappeared. "In front of us the way is seen," they cry, "but behind us the road is gone."
>
> (Ibid)

Had they not looked back, they would not have realized the disappearance of the road and would have put their lives in danger. Hence, looking back could save them. As the story goes, the king and the troops are enlightened by the knowledge imparted by the "*peréthaya*" who looks like "a deva," and the king wants to know how the *peréthaya* acquired such "splendor" despite his "miserly" nature in the past. *Peréthaya* explains the reason. Accordingly it is nothing but his daughter transferring the merits of her good deeds and generosity to her dead father (Ibid).

The story then is a message about a responsibility that goes beyond death. Had death made the daughter forget the father, had she failed to remember him, had she stopped looking back and recalled his past, everything would have ended between the two. Consequently, he would have suffered without having anyone to care for him and redeem him from the miserable state of a *peréthaya* by passing merits of good deeds to him.

Thus, the story of King Nandaka reminds him of the importance of looking back while moving ahead in search of freedom. It is both a responsibility and a necessity.

Yet, why should one bother to look back or care for the path that one walked, especially when "the way is seen" ahead? Looking the way ahead is important to the one who wants to go forward in life—progress. In such a progressive movement, taking the responsibilities for the dead might sound regressive. It could be seen as a waste of time, energy, and resources. Tabish Khair's *The Night of Happiness* (2018) dwells upon such responsibility to the dead, where he shows how the concerns for the dead could be mocked at and perceived as some sort of madness. Mr. Mehrotra's advice to Ahmed many days after the *halwa* incident on the day of *shraad e baraat* is all about such perceptions.

Looking back cannot be and should not be mandatory. Everyone should feel free to decide in this regard. Hence, in spite of the message that he got from the story of King Nandaka, Shivan too could continue his journey ahead without worrying about the past.

However, this time, Shivan seems to be worried. There are two questions in front of him: the first is the question of self-freedom; the second is about infinite responsibility to the other. These questions are, anyway, not new; they have appeared many times, and he kept choosing the one about which he is passionate—freedom. Then, the question is, why does he behave differently *this* time?

This time makes all the difference because this time is different from many other times. Yet, how could there be a different time other than the time already there? There is no *other* time other than this time. Good or bad, there is only one time. Whatever needs to be done should be done only within this time. Thus, there is no better time other than the one *already* here. Nevertheless, it took many years for Shivan to understand this reality. Had he realized this at least two years before, things would have been different from the way they are now. Now, there is no way to escape. While escaping, he has reached "the end" of his rope—*aporia*.

He says, "I was at the end of my rope, and there was nowhere to go except to the truth or its alternative, the end of our relationship" (Selvadurai 2013, 336).

In any case, neither of them affirms his freedom. He is unaware of the consequences followed by his decision. To decide in a moment when no decision is possible is to remain unconditionally open up to the outside/other. It is dangerous; he should sacrifice the thing he had cherished so far in front of the responsibility to the other. This time, he should face reality by revealing the truth, which is the truth about *The Hungry Ghosts* —the relationship with the other.

Who Are The Hungry Ghosts?

Stories about hungry ghosts were narrated to Shivan by his grandmother and mother during his childhood. Shivan remembers some of them till date. Moreover, by now, he too has his own story of such a ghost, though it is quite different due to the directional and positional changes (which we would discuss later). According to what he had heard, hungry ghosts are the ones who are reborn as *peréthayas* after death.

> In Sri Lankan myth, a person is reborn a peréthaya because, during his life, he desired too much—hence the large stomach that can never be filled through the tiny mouth. The peréthayas that appear to us are always our ancestors, and it is our duty to free them from their suffering by feeding Buddhist monks and transferring the merit of that deed to our dead relatives.
>
> (Ibid, 24–25)

Shivan's mother has seen such *peréthaya* of her husband in her dream. The dream keeps coming to her time and again since his death. In this dream,

> she encounters him at my grandmother's gate or standing by a pillar on the verandah or sometimes outside the market. He is reborn as a peréthaya, a hungry ghost, with stork-like limbs and an enormous belly that he must prop up with his hands. The yellowed flesh of his face is seared to the skull, his mouth no large than the eye of a needle, so he can never satisfy his hunger. He just stands, staring at her, caught between worlds.
>
> (Ibid, 24)

According to Shivan's mother, there are two reasons for the visits of her dead husband's *peréthaya*: The first is "her anger" which, as she believes, caused his death; the second, her failure to "beg his forgiveness" or attempt some "companiable peace with him" (Ibid).

Meanwhile, Shivan's grandmother, who also had stories of *peréthayas*, identifies herself with one of them: "Naked peréthi" (Ibid, 77), the unfortunate woman, "marooned on an island, surrounded by so much that is good in life but unable to enjoy it. Everything she touched, everything she loved, disintegrated in her hands" (Ibid).

However, unlike grandmother, Shivan's mother does not feel of herself as a *peréthaya*. It is about her dead husband. Yet, she is the cause for this unfortunate rebirth of him. The ghost reminds her of *her* guilt. It is true that he appears as *peréthaya* due to some unfulfilled desire that he had when he was alive. According to Buddhism, it is the effect of *karma*. But, it, in its appearance, reminds the living about his/her guilt, failure, or delay. It is this appearance of the disappeared and the disappearance that compels her to question herself regarding the death of the other. She cannot ignore it, nor could she postpone it. She is already late, causing the death to suffer. It is her responsibility to redeem him by giving him what he had desired. However, death does not allow her to give anything to him directly. She could give him only by giving to some other. It is an indirect way of doing things. This option of giving, passing, or transferring something via some other is enabled by religion. Religion facilitates such possibilities of connecting two worlds together: the world of the dead and that of the living. Hence, whatever to be done from her side in relation to the dead would be done in the *name* of the other.

Now, one might consider such practice of responsibility after death to be useless, meaningless, or absolutely foolish because no responsibility whatsoever could undo the death and bring the dead back to life. It is the impossible par excellent. In that sense, it also suggests, on the other hand, the necessity of being responsible for the other *prior* to death, reminding us of the moral imperative: *You shall not kill.*[16] This imperative for abstention from murder informs two things. One, it, implicitly though, affirms the ultimate capacity of our power exercisable over another, saying, implying *You could kill another*; *you shall kill another*. Second, it demands limiting such destructive power. The other is the limit to our power, capacity, and freedom. Then, the responsibility of the self to the other is always *already* prior to death.

Though self-questioning cannot reverse the event—death, though it might not have any impact on the dead, it makes one realize the unavoidable presence of the other within the self—*differànce*. It is necessary, one acknowledges its otherness, and this responsibility comes to self via the other. It starts from the other. To be responsible to the self is to be responsible to the other. Shivan's mother comes to this realization only after her husband's death. Had she already known this twist in responsibility, she would have had a different approach to her life with the husband and whatever the difference in the approach would have had a different effect not only on her life but also on everyone else related to her, though it is difficult to judge what that effect would be like and would do. On the other side, had her life unfolded in a different way other than how it actually *did*, she would not have heard the call for the responsibility like how she is hearing it now; also, she would not have understood the consequences of anger and hate, as well as, the urgency for peace and the necessity of forgiveness for making peace.

However, she cannot share this realization with Shivan in order to make him realize what it is like to be responsible since it is *her* realization—singularity. Yet, it is only by sharing that she could take care of her son and his future, which is yet another responsibility both as a human and as a mother. She keeps trying regardless of the repeated failures due to his efforts to ignore her and escape to Vancouver. In her attempt to be there for him, she keeps opening to his response, enduring the harshness in it.

This is what the mother has been trying to do for her son. But, what about the son? Is he able to realize how affectionate she is?

It is impossible for him to understand his mother. She is (an)other. The otherness of the mother does not allow complete understanding. If he manages to understand her completely, she would not be there anymore as (m) other. She would be totally absorbed, consumed, and exhausted in a manner that she is no more there *to be* or *to become*. Hence, it is necessary that understanding always remains at the level of an effort so that it continues as an infinite process. Then, he should *try* to understand her. The effort should come from him. Unless he makes it, the relationship remains absolutely asymmetrical.

Unfortunately, Shivan is reluctant to try this laborious and tedious task. Of course, it is not an interesting job! We are often interested in doing only the things which are of our interest.

What the mother is interested in doing is not of *his* interest, because she does not do what interests him. She instead does the opposite of what he does—taking responsibility. She has been *trying* without ever being able to succeed in any of the three roles: daughter, wife, and mother. Contrastingly, Shivan holds others responsible for his life and passes the responsibility to another. That is the easiest thing to do when one wants to *escape*. Till now, no one has confronted him with what he does. No one has questioned him because no one got the chance to do so.

But, this time, the mother has come to remind him of his responsibility, which he cannot pass onto another and escape. She places a request-cum-suggestion in front of him. It concerns truth, fidelity, responsibility, and justice in love. The conversation goes as follows:

> "I am guessing that Michael doesn't know anything about what happened, probably doesn't even know you have a grandmother. You have kept it all from that poor man."
>
> I fiddled in my pockets as if looking for something.
>
> She sat down and clasped her hands, staring at me. "It's not fair, Shivan. He deserves better."
>
> "Just keep out of my relationship," I snarled.

> "We should have stayed on campus," she said wretchedly.
>
> "You should have. Instead of which you've come and shat all over my happiness. Yes, *shat*," I cried, at my mother's shock. "I was happy. Why did you have to come and ruin everything? Haven't you done enough damage to my life?"
>
> (Ibid, 330)

This situation places a few questions before us: why does Shivan shout at his mother? Why does he think that she has *only* damaged him? Is he blind to her concern, love, and care? How could he behave toward his mother rudely and violently?

But is it a condition peculiar to Shivan? Is he the only one who behaves like that?

Stories in the novel show that it is not peculiar to Shivan; rather, it is the peculiarity of everyone—his mother, grandmother, sister, Mili, Michael, Chandralal, and so on. All of them are violent. The difference lies in how it appears because it could always appear differently in multiple ways and forms. It could range from speech to silence; action to inaction; light to darkness, aggression to sadness, laugh to tear, and activity to passivity (Derrida 1978, 97–192). Accordingly, even the most caring act, gesture, word, or look cannot be devoid of violence. This paradox and conflict could be seen in every relationship that appears in the novel. And it, in turn, urges us to philosophize whether at all there could be any relationship without violence.

Every relationship is found upon violence. No relation is possible *without* violence. However, we do not start relationships to be violent or enact violence, but to love and to care. Later is our intention. The problem here is whether the intention could be well communicated to the other and whether it would be well received by the other. On the other hand, even if the intention is good and well communicated, what if the approach is not so good, loving, and caring? That is why love and care always need to be attempted with utmost attentiveness so that they do not slip from the intention and thereby becoming the most violent.

Notes

1 Question of violence in Sri Lanka has been the central problem in my PhD dissertation titled " Religion, Nation, and Gender: A Study of the Problematic of Representation and Violence in the Context of Sri Lankan Literature." submitted to Center for Linguistics, School of Language, Literature, & Culture Studies, Jawaharlal Nehru University, New Delhi, 2016. I acknowledge that some of the concepts which appear in this book are discussed at length in the dissertation, and I have provided the due reference to the same in this book.

2 *The Hungry Ghosts* by Shyam Selvadurai was first published by Penguin Books India in 2013 by arrangement with Westwood Creative Artists Ltd. I acknowledge and thank the author, Shyam Selvadurai, the publisher, Penguin Books India, and the Westwood Creative Artists for allowing me to quote from their material in this book.

3 The Levinasian idea of the death and the other is important for the understanding of the notion of event. As Levinas explains in *Totality & Infinity: An Essay on Exteriority*, tr. Alphonso Lingis (Pennsylvania: Duquesne University Press, 1969) self is vulnerably exposed to the undecidable and unpredictable other. Since the other comes from the zone where death comes, the self neither could be aware of it nor could prevent its coming. It comes at its own will, which Derrida projects as the decision of the other. Moreover, coming of the other, event, cannot be prevented. See Jacques Derrida, *Politics of Friendship*, tr. George Collins (London: Verso, 1997). *Negotiations: Interventions and Interviews, 1971 – 2001*, ed. & tr. Elizabeth Rotternberg (California: Stanford University Press, 2002b). *The Gift of Death*, tr. David Wills (Chicago: The University of Chicago Press, 1995a). Maurice Blanchot's literary and philosophical works deal with the Levinasian idea of coming of the other as event. According to Blanchot, event is disastrous. It dismantles everything—violent. For a deeper understanding in this regard, see Maurice Blanchot, "Thomas the Obscure" in *The Station Hill Blanchot Reader: Fiction & Literary Essays*, ed. George Quasha, tr. Lidiya Davis et al (Barrytown: Station Hill Press, 1999), 51–128. , *The Writing of the Disaster*, tr. Ann Smock (Lincoln: University of Nebraska Press, 1995b).

4 Here, I foreground the significant aspect of language, which is addressing. It maintains that addressing as the possibility of language. Peggy Kamuf's *Book of Addresses* (California: Stanford University Press, 2005) provides great insights in this regard.

5 Emmanuel Levinas, *Totality & Infinity: An Essay on Exteriority*, tr. Alphonso Lingis (Pennsylvania: Duquesne University Press, 1969). *Otherwise than Being or Beyond Essence*, tr. Alphonso Lingis (Netherlands: Kluwer Academic Publishers, 1991); Maurice Blanchot, *The Space of Literature*, tr. Ann Smock (Lincoln: University of Nebraska Press, 1982). *Work of Fire*, tr. Charlotte Mandell (California: Stanford University Press, 1995a); Jacques Derrida, *The Ear of the Other: Otobiography, Transference, Translation*, tr. Peggy Kamuf (New York: Schocken Books, 1985). *The Politics of Friendship*, tr. George Collins (London: Verso, 1997). *Monolingualism of the Other or The Prosthesis of Origin*, tr. Patrick Mensah (California: Stanford University Press, 1998). *The Work of Mourning*, ed. Pascale Anne Brault, Michael Naas (Chicago: The University of Chicago Press, 2001a). *On Touching—Jean-Luc Nancy*, tr. Christine Irizarry (California: Stanford University Press, 2005); Peggy Kamuf, *Book of Addresses* (California: Stanford University Press, 2005).

6 This idea slightly contrasts with that of Deleuze and Gauthari in *A Thousand Plateaus: Capitalism and Schizophrenia* (London: University of Minnesota Press, 1987) where they suggest that writing happens not when one is not able to say I, but when it is no longer important to say I. Accordingly, the idea in the present work highlights the vulnerable condition of the self, where it is unable to find its own self without the presence of the other. If it is such an inability, it cannot be so much about the importance. Rather, it could be otherwise. Even if one wants to say I, even one finds the importance of saying I, one is unable to do so due to the "distractedness" or helplessness, which is, according to Blanchot, "the intrusion of the other". Blanchot and Helence Cixous present this fatal condition of writ-

ing by referring to Franz Kafka and Clarice Lispector. Maurice Blanchot, *The Space of Literature*, tr. Ann Smock (Lincoln: University of Nebraska Press, 1982), *Work of Fire*, tr. Charlotte Mandell (California: Stanford University Press, 1995); Helene Cixous, *Three Steps on the Ladder of Writing*, tr. S. Cornell (New York: Columbia University Press, 1993). Further, Peggy Kamuf discusses this idea of "shift" or "displacement" from I to he/she/it in "'Fiction' and the Experience of the Other," in *Book of Address* (California: Stanford University Press, 2005), 135–153.

However, explaining the fictional movement where the impossibility of appropriating or "equating" the voice of the characters with that of the writer, Peggy Kamuf evokes certain radicalness in fiction. She suggests the possibility of understanding fiction as "whatever may arise from the essential possibility of saying "I" and meaning another, or alternatively of saying "he" or "she" without being able to exclude a reference to self." For further knowledge in this regard, refer to "Deconstruction Reading Politics: Democracy's Fiction (Everything, Anything, and Nothing at All)," in *Book of Address* (California: Stanford University Press, 2005), 172–188.

7 I acknowledge that this discussion, yet in a detailed manner, appears in my PhD thesis titled "Religion, Nation, and Gender: A Study of the Problematic of Representation and Violence in the Context of Sri Lankan Literature", which was submitted to the Center for Linguistics, School of Language, Literature & Culture Studies, Jawaharlal Nehru University, New Delhi in 2016.

8 As an example, Sri Lankan Sinhala Buddhists perform certain rituals *in the name of* the dead. They invite Buddhist monks to chant *pirith* (overnight chating of some *sutras*) or *bana* (sermons limited to an hour or two in the evening) at the house of the diseased, then offer *danas* (alms giving) to them, as well as to those who have come to share the grief of the mourning family. It is necessary to begin these rituals in the evening of the sixth day and complete them by the afternoon of the seventh day after the death. In Sri Lanka, it is known as "hathdavase daane" (seventh-day almsgiving). The same ritual is repeated on the day completing three months from the death, known as "thunmaase daane" (three months' almsgiving). However, often, a close relative of the dead continues in offering *daana* to a Buddhist monk in the nearby temple monthly and transfers merits of the good deed to the dead even after the three months' ritual.

The ritual called "śrāddha" practiced among the Hindus is another example. For further knowledge, refer to Dakshinaranjan Shastri, *Origin and Development of the Rituals of Ancestor Worship in India* (Calcutta: Bookland Private Limited, 1963); Gian Giuseppe Flippi, *Mṛtyu: Concept of Death in Indian Traditions: Transformation of the Body and Funeral Rites* (New Delhi: D.K. Printworld, 1996).

9 This idea is central to Derrida's philosophy. Though almost all his works discuss this idea, it appears prominently in some of the following works: Jacques Derrida et al., "A Number of Yes (Nombre de oui)," *Qui Parle: Silence and Intervention* 2, no. 2 (1988): 118–133, http://www.jstor.org/stable/20713732. *Ethics, Institutions, and the Right to Philosophy*, ed. & tr. Peter Pericles Trifonas (Maryland: Rowman & Littlefield Publishers, 2002c). *Negotiations: Interventions and Interviews, 1971–2001*, ed. & tr. Elizabeth Rotternberg (California: Stanford University Press, 2002b). *Of Hospitality: Anne Doufermantlle Invites Jacques Derrida Respond*, tr. Rachel Bowlby (California: Stanford University Press, 2000).

10 See the critiques of Freudian and Lacanian theory of psychoanalysis by Jacques Derrida, Maurice Blanchot, Michel Foucault, and Gilles Deleuze and Félix Guattari.

11 It is the case with most of the Sri Lankan Sinhalese and Tamils. See Gananath Obeyesekere quoted in Stanley Jeyaraja Tambiah, *Sri Lanka: Ethnic Fratricide and the Dismantling of Democracy* (Delhi: Oxford University Press, 1986).

12 Sections 365 and 365a in the Sri Lankan Penal Code. For further knowledge, please refer to "Sri Lanka: Types of Criminalization." Accessed December 08, 2021. https://www.humandignitytrust.org/country-profile/sri-lanka/; "Sri Lanka: Forced Anal Exams in Homosexuality Prosecutions: Police, Judicial Officers Should End Arbitrary Arrests, Torture of LGBT People." Accessed December 08, 2021. https://www.hrw.org/news/2020/10/20/sri-lanka-forced-anal-exams-homo sexuality-prosecutions; "Sri Lanka Laws Proscribing Homosexual Acts and Whether They Are Applied in Practice; The Treatment by Authorities, by Society at Large and by the Muslim Community." Accessed December 08, 2021. https://www.refworld.org/docid/47ce6d7d2d.html ; "Sri Lanka LGBT Resources." Accessed September 07, 2021. https://www.refugeelegalaidinfo rmation.org/sri-lanka-lgbti-resources; "All Five Fingers Are Not the Same": Discrimination on Grounds of Gender Identity and Sexual Orientation in Sri Lanka." Accessed September 07, 2021. https://www.hrw.org/report/2016/08/16/all-five-fingers-are-not-same/discrimination-grounds-gender-identity-and-sexual.

13 Commenting on attitudes to the homeland in South Asian Canadian Literature, Makarand Paranjape offers a critical perspective on the relationship between diasporas and homelands. See Makarand R. Paranjape, "One Foot in Canada and a Couple of Toes in India: Diasporas and Homelands in South Asian Canadian Experience," in *In Diaspora: Theories, Histories, Texts* (New Delhi: Indialog Publications, 2001), 161–169.

14 The case of Salman Rushdie, Tasleema Nazreen, also recent incidents of murdering bloggers in Bangladesh are some incidents which bring forth the danger of the freedom of expression.

15 See Jacques Derrida's discussion on the ontological question formed in terms of "what" in *Margins of Philosophy*, tr. Alan Bass (Sussex: The Harvester Press, 1982).

16 This idea is found almost in all religions in the world. In Buddhism, this is the first precept, which should be followed by every human regularly: "*pānāthi pātā veramani sikkā padan samādiyāmi.*" The one who observes this precept promises to refrain from murder.

2

VIOLENCE

Love and Hospitality

Michael wants to hear *the* truth from Shivan *only* if Shivan loves him; also *only* if he values the life that they have built together. Truth is important only if one loves the other. If it is otherwise, the truth could be optional.

Shivan and Michael have been in love for the last two years. He is filled with awe and gratitude for the life offered to him by Michael (Selvadurai 2013, 314). However, Michael's request to Shivan implies that Michael is not certain about Shivan's love. Suddenly, he is uncertain about his love: whether he loves him *truly*. This day that comes after two years of love is a different day in their relationship. It is a day of uncertainty. But, isn't it the case with *every* day? Every day comes with uncertainty as if uncertainty is the only thing it could bring by coming every day—as if it comes only to bring that or remind us about that. Uncertainty is the only certainty of every day, also of every minute. That is why we try to make things certain. What we build is always a building against uncertainty, as well as a building of uncertainty. Therefore, every building, every construction is to collapse at any time. *The Last Word* of Blanchot speaks about collapsing buildings (1999, 35–50). Yet, when we build, when we are in the process, we tend to forget that it is a building standing on and against uncertainty. We try our best to make it indestructible. Moreover, we believe that the building is indestructible, for we have taken adequate steps to make it strong. That is how all the owners think about what they have built. And, "it is natural" for the owners to think, "it is indestructible and that it won't fall down" (Ibid, 49).

Michael also has such a building with Shivan—their relationship. They have built it together, thinking that it would last. It belongs to both of them, and both should value it. For the last two years, Michael has been of the idea that Shivan values the co-building, though most of it has been built sitting in Michael's apartment, which he refers to as "my apartment" (Selvadurai 2013, 341, 354). He could choose to do anything that he likes *with* his apartment, also *in* his apartment. Shivan cannot question him regarding that (Ibid, 354). On the other hand, Shivan cannot do what he wants to do there without taking Michael's permission, as it is Michael's space and his

DOI: 10.4324/9781003045212-3

sovereignty. Nonetheless, it does not mean that Shivan does not have any freedom there. He has all the freedom so long as it does not disturb Michael, so long as it does not cross the limits set by Michael. They are *Michael's limits* on Shivan.

But has he actually put some limits or conditions on Shivan?

No. Not at all.

Till this day, which has come after many days of two years, he has not mentioned any condition. There was no need for him to put a condition. Things between them have been going well and smoothly.

However, Michael, being the owner of the flat in which he lived together with Shivan as lovers, had felt a sense of ownership not only towards the objects there but also to Shivan. In such a context, it is natural for Michael to feel, to believe, or to expect that Shivan should value their life. This is what *he* had thought, believed, and expected. But, today, due to some sudden unfolding of an event, the sense of certainty is shaken, and he is unable to be certain anymore about what he had felt.

What had he felt? What was he certain about?

Love.

Michael had felt love. It was the love of Shivan. He had felt that Shivan loves him. He was certain about it. All the days of two years had come to pass, assuring the certainty that Shivan loves him. Those days are different from today. Today makes all the difference as if the difference is the only thing that today bears to be different from the other two days—yesterday and tomorrow—one is gone; the other is *to come*.

The uncertainty appears in his request to Shivan. "Shivan, *if* you love me, *if* you value the life we have built together, I beg you to tell me the truth. The truth that you have hidden from me for as long as we've known each other" (Ibid, 336, italics added).

Michael is not able to request Shivan without putting the "if" condition. It is the condition of uncertainty. Otherwise, he could have made the request, without putting this conditional clause, "if." He could have talked to him affirmatively, like how one talks about facts. For example: Shivan, *since* you love me, *since* you value the life we have built together, I beg you to tell me the truth.

But, he does not say so, because he does not *know* whether Shivan loves him or values the life they have built together. How would he *know*? It is a sudden realization of his inability to *know* the other. He cannot assure the love of (an)other. It is the other's love that is undecidable. The only thing that he could do is to love the other, knowing that he loves the other. He has been doing so for the last two years. Yet, who knows? Who could exactly say whether he actually loves the other or whether his love is actually for the other?

There is no other who could know it better than Michael.

But, *what if* even he does not know?

At times, we are unaware of *what* we are doing while doing what we *want* to do. We, as the doers of action, assume that we *know* what we do. Yet, while doing it, we are ignorant of what is actually being done. There is some blindness within us, disenabling full vision. There is no better example other than love to understand this unavoidable ignorance of ours—Narcissism (Derrida on https://youtu.be/ya46wfeWqJk; De Armitt 2014, 91–140).

Michael's request for truth is a request *of* love. It entails two requests. One is the request for truth. The other is the request for love. Shivan should tell the truth only if he loves Michael. On the other hand, if he loves Michael, he should tell him *only* the truth. Here, truth is the expression of love; love is the expression of truth (Nalika 2019, 10).

Hence, Shivan is to speak in allegory.

He is to express his love for Michael, without saying *I love you*. Expressing love in these three words is the most difficult thing in love. On the other hand, it is difficult to express love without saying these three words. The expression of love—*I love you*—is thus paradoxical. One cannot love without expressing it. Love is to express. It expresses one's love for another—someone other than me or different from me. Therefore, it is also an expression from one to another expressing one's relationship with another. However, as mentioned above, expressing one's love for another is difficult. It is impossible. It is about expressing, speaking, telling, saying, and presenting the inexpressible. Then, the expression of love—*I love you*—always and already carries one's inability and dissatisfaction in the act of expressing. It is the only way to express the impossibility of expressing love—helplessness. Here, there are two kinds of helplessness: one is the impossibility to express love for another. The other is the one related to the feeling, love. Love is already a helpless condition where one is not able to manage without the other. The other should be there before me for me to be there. The other is the first priority (Levians 1969, 1991). In that sense, love is not *only* about me but also about me with the other.

Then, Shivan's condition is more vulnerable. He is already in love with Michael. That is why there is "nowhere to go except to the truth or its alternative, the end of our relationship." The alternative is unbearable. He is unable to manage his being without Michael. That is the truth, and there is no alternative to that truth. By agreeing to tell the truth under the request, he surrenders to *his* truth—the impossibility of the self without the other. It is this vulnerability, which makes him express the inexpressible. But there is another condition, which adds to the *already* difficult condition. That is, he is not allowed to express his love for Michael by saying, "I love you" (Nalika 2019, 11). Michael does not want to hear it anymore. What he wants to hear is the truth. By opening up to hear the truth that "had taken all his courage" (Selvadurai 2013, 336), he opens up to hear love. According to the conditioned request goes, "if you love me, if you value the life [...], I beg you to tell me the truth," whatever to be told by Shivan would be both truth and love for Michael. All these days, he has been hearing love for truth and love as truth but, today, he wants to hear the truth for love and truth as love. They are two different things. The former is comforting, consoling, and calming, while the latter is not necessarily so. It could be disturbing, weakening, damaging, and destructive because one could express one's love by revealing that he or she does not love the other: *I don't love you*. How paradoxical is this? That is why Michael's request becomes difficult; it is a very tricky one. When one opts to hear the truth, one is absolutely ignorant of the thing to be heard. The thirst for truth is thus dangerous as it exposes being to the unknown. It is decisive, and one needs all the courage to decide to hear the dangerous truth. And, Michael has taken this decision to face the danger.

However, when compared to Michael, Shivan's situation is worse. Michael needed only his courage to make the request. Once he managed to gather all strength, he was *able* to ask with the words supporting him to bring in the clarity. Yet, Shivan does not have that support, since he is not allowed to speak *the* truth that he knows *as* truth—his love for Michael. Instead, he should speak the truth that Michael wants to hear. There is a difference between what he wants Michael to hear and what Michael wants to hear from him. In any case, there is no space for him to put his desire first. Michael's request has already pre-empted that possibility. Hence, he should begin to speak what the other wants to hear. It is yet another problem.

How would he know what the other wants to hear?

It is impossible for him to be aware of that. Certainly, he knows that Michael needs to hear the truth. That, too, the one which is hidden from him since the time they came to know each other. According to Michael, Shivan has hidden the truth from him. Moreover, he knows that Shivan has a hidden truth. He says, "The truth that you have, I know now, hidden from me."

Shivan is unaware of the specific truth at demand because, for him, there are many truths in one truth. If he is to tell the truth, he should tell everything known to him as truth, for all of them are important. On the other hand, he is aware that Michael is not ready to listen to everything. He needs to hear only the one which is of his concern. However, the thing to be revealed as truth actually does not concern him. It is about some other. Unfortunately, he does not want to hear the thing, which actually concerns him.

Accordingly, there are two tasks in front of him. One is to tell the truth to prove his love. The other is to express his love for the other as the only truth. The former is the demand of the other; the latter is the desire for the other. He should addrress both at the same time. His expression should meet the needs of the other. It is made only to address the other. Meanwhile, he should also manage to express his desire.

Shivan should invent an expression that could do both. This crucial situation of Shivan reminds us of Echo, who wants to express her love to

Narcissus despite the injunction of God that governs Echo's speech, also life. This is the fate she is to endure. Nevertheless, as Derrida says, Echo does not give up her efforts (DeArmitt 2014, 91–140), because she cannot give up her love for Narcissus. She should try to express the inexpressible. Accordingly, "Echo, in her loving and infinite cleverness, arranges it so that in repeating the last syllables of the words of Narcissus, she speaks in such a way that the words become her own" (Ibid, 135).

Shivan begins to speak. He speaks about what he *could not* speak earlier. It was his inability to speak (Selvadurai 2013, 340). He did not know how to speak about it with Michael. The two opposite feelings in which his mind oscillated—wanting to share, yet not being able to share—have made him feel uncomfortable. Even though Michael's allegation against Shivan is about hiding the truth, it is not an act of hiding but failure in language. Language has not supported him to express what he wants to express. It ends up expressing in its way and communicates something other than the intended because it either says more or says less (Derrida 2005, 168). In that sense, there would be a betrayal of language, and it could have some negative influence on the relationship. All these days, he feared betrayal of any kind. For the last two years, he had guarded against it with all his strength to protect his love for Michael while valuing their relationship. Nevertheless, today, what he had protected has betrayed him and made him guilty for "hiding truth"; what he had feared and tried avoiding has taken place finally. The effort has been useless; he is guilty of betrayal. In fact, he has always been guilty of the same fault—betrayal of love.

Now, there is no time for him to think "how to speak." Time is up. He should speak without thinking. There is no art or craft that he could master in order to speak without a betrayal. Every work of art and craft is a work of betrayal (Blanchot 1999). It took two years for him to come to terms with this undeniable truth. Now, he is to speak without any guard. He places Mili's obituary gently on the bed, calling Michael (Selvadurai 2013, 336).

Violence in/of Obituary

It is Mili's obituary opened on the bed. By opening it, Shivan has exposed himself to Michael. That is what he could do. There is so much to say about the obituary, and all those were to do with Sri Lanka. Shivan had distanced himself from that land after Mili's death since it distanced Mili from him. The obituary was in his knapsack. That is where he had kept it folded when he tore it from the government-owned newspaper.

The newspaper article that had carried the story of Mili's death is lying in front of Shivan and Michael in this moment of revelation. Shivan has laid it down on the bed as if it is the truth. There is "a photograph of Mili from when he was a teenager, wearing our school tie and blazer, holding aloft a cricket trophy won under his captainship, grinning in that old, easy way" (Ibid, 244). Now, the image is "smudged" (Ibid, 336). It is the truth—the image. There is only an image of the one he had loved. That is not clear as much as how it appeared on the day it got published first. Then, it was soon after his death. It was an image on a fresh obituary. Now, it has become old; the image has already begun to blur. So soon!

One might see it as a problem of the poor-quality-print newspaper in the 1980s' Sri Lanka. During those days, the Sri Lankan newspapers were of poor quality, not so much in terms of the materials for printing but of reporting. It was poor reporting. But, reporting is anyway poor; it has always been and will continue to be poor. That is why there are many reports about the same thing, incident, event, place, people, etc.; also, there are many newspapers which report the same thing in many different ways. In that sense, they all are about impossible reporting. While reporting, they also report the impossibility of reporting. It is also like translation (Derrida 1985, 93–161, 2002a, 105–134). And, it is not a peculiar case of Sri Lankan newspapers, but about all newspapers.

However, when reporting is thus *already* a difficult task, just imagine reporting in Sri Lanka in the days of the 1980s! Most of the newspapers were owned by the then government in Sri Lanka. Things to be reported during those days were so bizarre that the government needed to have control over reporting. Reporting with no control or censorship exposes everything, including the government. Generally, governments do not like to be absolutely exposed. They enjoy exposure only to the things with which they are comfortable; they seek exposure only for the things that they want to expose to the public. The rest should be known only to the government. And, the public is also aware that some of the things about the government known by the public are probably those which the government did not want them to know. Hence, as a way of respecting the government, especially because of fear, some people pretended to be ignorant. Those were the days all the Sri Lankans were fear stricken. Sinhalese, Tamils, and Muslims, as well as other ethnic groups—all were scared. No group could escape fear because there were three groups which had taken control over every other group. On the one side, there were Tamil Tiger rebels known as Liberation of Tamil Eelam (LTTE). They majorly operated from the North of Sri Lanka. On the other side, there was Janatha Vimukthi Peramuna (JVP), a radical Marxist group basically known to have operated from the South, though they were operative from South to North Central of Sri Lanka. Above all, there was the government struggling against the two.

Post-independent Sri Lanka saw the rising tides of antagonism between Sinhalese and Tamils. By the mid-1950s, riots began to erupt in different parts of the country. Since childhood, Shyam's Shivan has been aware of this "escalating tension" (Selvadurai 2013, 63) between the two groups. Commenting on Sri Lanka's first decades of independence, Shyam writes,

> While the first decades of independence had brought a national flowering on many fronts, these decades also saw the beginning of ethnic tension between Sinhalese and Tamils, leading to the communal riots in 1956 and again in 1958, when many Tamils lost their lives, homes and livelihood. During the 1970s, ethnic tension continued to grow between Sinhalese and Tamils. There were riots in 1977 again in 1981 in which more Tamils lost lives and property. From the late '70s, the Liberation of Tamil Eelam (LTTE) became the dominant Tamil political voice, demanding a separate state and resorting to increased violence in order to get this separate country. Finally, the tension boiled over in the July 1983 riots.
>
> (Selvadurai 2014, xx–xxi)

However, until 1983, Colombo remained comparatively unaffected except for some curfews. When Shivan was growing into his teens,

> the rebels began to bomb state institutions, rob banks and kill policemen. In retaliation, the government passed Prevention of Terrorism Act, which allowed them to make arrests without warrants hold a person indefinitely without laying a charge, use confessions made under duress as admissible evidence and dispose of bodies without an inquest.
>
> (Selvadurai 2013, 63)

Finally, July 1983 put Colombo in flames. Colombo riots were the consequences of previous incidents of violence done by the both Sri Lankan army and the LTTE provoking each other. Therefore, there is no point in asking who did what and who did it first because there was never a First with so much clarity. One could go on searching the origin of this violence with the help of some historical accounts. Yet, how much could history be of any help in the problem of violence when the history itself is not absolved from the violence (Derrida 1978, 97–192)? There is no history of pure violence because history itself cannot be pure from violence (Derrida 1994). Nevertheless, both the groups took provocation as the best way to address each other in order to meet their demands. While provoking each other, they also ended up provoking the civilians of both sides against each other. Riots are consequences of such provocations while being provocative to provoke one against another. Accordingly, during Black July, Sinhalese civilians were provoked against Tamils (Hoole 2001).

When Shivan heard this story on July 25th, he and his sister were having breakfast sitting at his grandmother's home in Colombo. That is where he, his sister, and his mother have been living since his childhood. Though it was not an easy life due to the constant verbal fights and arguments between his mother and the grandmother, they had to bear that life as there was no other safe and affordable option. Hema, Shivan's mother, had lost her husband and become a widow at a young age (Selvadurai 2013, 21). Until the death of their father, Shivan and Renu had not heard about a grandmother.

> "We have an aachi?" Renu tucked in her chin, incredulous.
> "Yes, of course, did you think I was born in a rubbish bin?"
> "But, why haven't we met this aachi?" I asked.
> "Because," my mother paused for emphasis, "she hates you."
> We stared at her dumbfounded. "Why?" Renu finally demanded.
> "Because you are half Tamil. Your grandmother did not want me to marry your father because he was Tamil. And now that you are half Tamil, she hates you."
>
> (Ibid, 20)

The (un)fortunate death of their father had finally brought three of them to the grandmother's house. The financially broken condition had forced them to depend on the grandmother, who was rich and dominant. Nevertheless, despite the refugee status of Hema at her mother's house, she continued her years-old resentment with her mother.

How could she be so demanding and dictating as a refugee? Is she allowed to behave like that? Does she have a right to argue, demand, or disagree especially with the one who has provided her with a safe and comfortable shelter? Withholding these questions to be discussed later in the chapter, let's get back to this scene of the Black July.

It was Rosalind who told them about the terrible incident which had happened at the Kanaththa in the evening of the previous day—burying the bodies of the 13 murdered soldiers at the Kanaththa Cemetery and a reaction of a mob gathered at the funeral. They had "fanned out through the neighbourhood, burning Tamil houses and killing Tamil people" (Ibid, 64).

Riots are about unleashing violence and vengeance against each other. They could be calmed down only by the powerful intervention of the state with immediate and effective measures involving armed security forces and police. Civilians could expect help only from the state. But, what if the state itself gets involved in such a thing? In such a situation, where would people go? From whom could they expect help?

There was no one to intervene and quench the flame when the Colombo riots erupted in July 1983. In fact, such intervention was not necessary, because those who got involved in it were poised to accomplish the role assigned to them by hook or by crook. They seemed to have taken all the necessary steps to keep it going until they met their desired end—teaching a lesson to Tamils by attacking them and destroying their houses. The mob had targeted only Tamils. If not so, how could a frenzied mob manage so accurately in selecting only the Tamil houses amid the riots in a place like Colombo? Colombo, being the city of Sri Lanka, is inhabited by all ethnicities in large numbers. Sinhalese, Tamils, Muslims, and Eurasians are spread everywhere in the city depending on their financial credibility. Therefore, it is not easy, especially for a mob, to isolate a Tamil house from other houses.

Shivan's grandmother's house was just a ten-minute car ride from the cemetery. The mob could easily reach there. However, until Chandralal spoke about what he had heard from others, Shivan's mother was with the idea, "surely the government will act to stop it."

> I've heard rumors that certain members of government are behind the rioting. The funeral mob, it seems, was armed with electoral lists telling them which houses were Tamil [...] These members of government say that they are sick of the Tigers and wanted to teach Tamils a lesson.
>
> (Ibid, 64)

If any Tamil family managed to escape attacks, it was due to either some help extended to them by a Sinhalese or some connections that one must have had with an influential politician of the then government. In any case, the second option was possible only for those who were very rich. Richness alone must not have become a qualification for them to be saved from the mob. Additionally, their political alignment, too, must have mattered. However, there were some Sinhalese, who had managed to save the lives of their Tamil friends by hiding them in their houses and protecting them till the situation became normal. Shivan's grandmother herself is one of such Sinhalese, who had saved a Tamil family from Wellawatte during the riots. Yet, her way of helping was different. It was a *deal* rather than a help. As Chandralal protected it for "a cheaper house price," the house standing on the street in Wellawatte remained unharmed. Chandralal and grandmother had made a deal with that family (Ibid, 217–218).

That is sad; yet, at least those people were not killed.

The Wellawatte property deal by Chandralal and Shivan's grandmother is just one incident that appears in the novel. But, considering Colombo's Wellawatte as a locality mostly populated by Tamils, it echoes the cry of Tamils frantically trying to escape death. And, there must have been many, like Chandralal and the grandmother, who made hay out of the vulnerable situation of another.

However, the problem is whether such people see themselves as opportunists.

Everyone's understanding of their actions is determined by how they *want* to see, read, interpret, and understand them. Often, it is in favour of one's (own) self. When Shivan confronted his grandmother regarding the property, she projects hers and Chandralal's help as the best thing that could happen to the family. She says,

> That family had three teenage daughters. The mob would have turned those girls into soiled goods, then murdered them. [...] Chandralal saved them from all that. He put his reputation, his golayas, his own life, at stake. What is that compared to a cheaper house price? [...] Now look at that family. They have a new life in Australia, a better life than here. Those girls [...] will be prime candidates in the bridal market. [...] We gave them a fair deal, we gave them their lives.
>
> (Ibid, 217–218)

If the target behind the riot was to teach a lesson to Tamils, it was not an entirely new lesson to them. They had been learning different lessons from Sinhala politicians. Knee-jerk turns taken by the Sri Lankan governments in post-independent Sri Lanka in the attempt of making it a Sinhala Buddhist nation had adversely affected Tamil. LTTE itself is a repercussion of those insensitive and discriminatory steps.[1]

Since the riots broke out, Tamils had been running for their lives. Some ran within the island; some fled outside. Those who managed to migrate[2] to other parts of the world had a different set of problems, including, as Shyam writes, "the daily contempt of white people" (Selvadurai 2013, 218). They were refugees, asylum seekers. On the other hand, migration to other countries, other than to India, was not an easy accomplishment. Yet, one is ready to face hardships to save his/her life. So, they must have managed life like how Shivan and his family did in Canada.

However, the majority of Tamils had no option other than to stay in Sri Lanka. Among them, the plight of those stuck in Jaffna and other areas in North and North-east was more miserable. They were the victims of all sorts of violence unleashed by the LTTE and Sri Lankan Army on an everyday basis.[3] Even if LTTE claimed to have fought for the protection of Tamils in Sri Lanka, many Tamils feared the LTTE as well. I wonder, let alone the fear and contempt that they had felt towards the Sri Lankan Army and the government, how many Tamils, who experienced the intense fights in the North, could agree with violence committed by the LTTE in the name of Eelam.

Thus, neither the government nor the LTTE could bring them some respite. Those trapped in the war zone had become refugees and hostages at the same time. Though other Tamils, who lived in the other parts of the country populated by Sinhalese and Muslims, too, had to undergo pressure, their condition was considerably better. At least, they were not deprived of their necessities, like water, food, and electricity, as well as buying their daily needs for the usual price in the market, getting school education to their children, the access to free health care, and managing whatever the jobs that they had and earning a salary. Most importantly, they did not have to bear the pain of LTTE carders taking their children by force to train and recruit them as LTTE carders. If one had some shelter and a small job, one could manage life despite the fear and guilt. The fear was due to the ethnicity vulnerable to arbitrary arrests by the state security forces under the Act of Prevention of Terrorism. The sense of guilt and shame in the eyes of Sinhalese and other ethnic groups in Sri Lanka is due to the casualties and destruction brought by blasts carried out by the LTTE suicide bombers. LTTE had projected every violent step taken by them as an attempt to assure the freedom of Tamils. Hence, every Tamil was to bear their indirect connection and contribution to the ongoing violence of terrorism, even when they have not taken part in any act of terrorism (Munaweera 2013).

Meanwhile, as mentioned in the first chapter, Sri Lanka during the 1970s–1990s was grappling with the other main issue in the island—the Marxist movement led by JVP. In 1971, JVP had operated their first armed revolt against the then Sri Lankan government under Prime Minister Sirimavo Bandaranaike. "The Che Guervarist insurgency of 1971 revealed the bitter disaffection of the young and unemployed" (Kemper 1991, 165). It was a well-planned yet failed attempt said to have happened due to the lack of communication (Fernando 2013, April 1971 JVP). Hence, it could not seize power. However, the defeat could not bring the death knell to the party and its mission. The second phase of its history, which begins after 1971, is, as Gamini Keerawella points out, "the so-called 'Social Democratic' phase, during which the JVP tried to "enter into the mainstream of parliamentary politics," though "it was not clear whether the JVP genuinely adopted the parliamentary path or whether it was merely a tactical move latter became the strategy and the end itself." However, since the Jayawardene regime from 1977 could not address the socio-economic problems increased, especially during the post-1977 political developments in the country, the JVP was able to emerge "as the main force" capable of challenging the government in a violent manner (Keerawella 1995, 150). It managed to gain the support of students, unemployed youth, oppressed caste elements, young Buddhist monks, and army deserters (Ibid, 164). The tendency to JVP become such an influential force in the country was also determined by its linkage with Sinhala nationalistic activities, which were anti-Tamil by nature (Ibid, 161).

JVP's Sinhala nationalistic, anti-Tamil ideology grew more aggressive and violent in the context of the Indo-Lanka Peace Accord, July 1987. As Shyam writes, India had to intervene due to the "pressure from its massive Tamil population in the sub-continent's south" (Selvadurai 2013, 138). Consequently, under the 1987 Indo–Sri Lankan Accord signed between Sri

Lanka and India, India sent its Indian Peace Keeping Army (IPKA) to Tamil areas in the North in order to end the civil war between the LTTE and the Sri Lankan military. Though the Tigers had agreed "reluctantly" to the truce that came as support from India, soon there were major disagreements between the two, for LTTE did not want to be disarmed, even if it was a prerequisite to peace. However, within three months, the LTTE broke the truce and killed five Indian para-commandos by strapping burning tyres around their necks (Ibid). Nevertheless, fearing the potency of Tamil autonomy in the Northern region, the JVP did not like India's presence in the North. It staged its protest openly against the Accord, highlighting India's intention to occupy Sri Lanka. Accordingly, it was a "Patriotic War to liberate the motherland from Indian occupation" in which the JVP began a "patriotic war" against the then government led by President J.R. Jayawardene (Keerawella 1995, 165). They attacked security force camps; staged daring robberies; declared strikes no one dared disobey (Selvadurai 2013, 139). As Shyam writes, "their power was so universally acknowledged that they were known as the Government of the Night or the Little Government" (Ibid).

On the other hand, the government was very determined to crush the JVP by using all possible strategies. It "secretly" formed a Sinhalese paramilitary unit called "the Green Tigers" to hunt and kill suspected JVP activists every day (Ibid, 158) while adopting various methods to malign the JVP so that the public disdain them. Accordingly, the JVP was recognized as the culprit behind many crimes committed in the 1980s and 1990s, especially in the areas spread from the South to the North. Black July itself is one of such massive incidents, and the government made the JVP one of the responsible parties for the same (Eleanor on https://www.sciencespo.fr/mass-violence-war-massacre-resistance/en/document/massacres-sri-lanka-during-black-july-riots-1983; Keerawella 1995).

Thus, no one was better than another. All three groups found their success by killing the enemy. Moreover, each group was an enemy of every other group; every group, accordingly, had two other rival groups. That provided a favourable ground for the game of continuous abductions, disappearances, and killings. It was a dangerous, funny, and ridiculous mechanism with no rule of law. In Shyam's terms, it was a "banana republic" (Selvadurai 2013, 204). The government did not mind the JVP killing Tamils or vice versa, for they both continued to threaten and cripple the government in many different ways. Probably, the government enjoyed watching the rivalry. On the other hand, the LTTE was not bothered by what was going on among Sinhalese divided by the left-wing and the right-wing politics. The United National Party (UNP) party members agreed and supported the government's initiatives against the JVP. Sri Lanka Freedom Party (SLFP), the left-wing main opposition, too, did not show much resistance to the same. There were opportunists as well, who used and manipulated this situation taking revenge from their personal enemies. Accordingly, one could secretly inform the police or some UNP henchmen about his/her rival as a supporter of the JVP. This snippet of information alone was adequate to bring the disaster to the rival or his/her family. Rather than the political inclination, it was the jealousy, hypocrisy, and hate felt for the success, happiness, and education of another, which were behind the many incidents of disappearance, abductions, arrests, and killings during that time. The JVP could neither side with the LTTE nor could it do with the government since, for them, they were simply the enemy of the Sri Lankan state and the Sinhala nation. They were irritated with whoever was sympathetic to Tamils. As an example, they murdered Vijay Kumaratunga, a Sinhala cinema veteran actor-turned-politician. Shyam projects this murder as "the most notorious crime" done by the JVP. It had declared him as a "traitor" for he was "sympathetic" to the Tamils (Ibid, 139).

Nevertheless, coming back to the obituary, the newspaper article reporting Mili's death is also from the same era. It was a government-owned newspaper, which had reported "quotes" from fishermen "confirming" strong currents that night, which led to the postponement of the funeral until the body was found (Ibid, 244).

Hospitality and Violence

In 1988, Shivan decided to visit his sick grandmother in Sri Lanka. That was his first visit after four years since he landed in Canada. However, the mother did not want him to go back to Sri Lanka, nor did she want him to visit the grandmother. Yet, Shivan wanted to visit her because she is family and "despite everything," she has been good to them. He remembers her "hospitality" extended to three of them when they had gone to her doorstep. Moreover, their life in Canada has become a bit comfortable because of the rent-free house that they managed to get due to her generosity and love for Shivan (Ibid, 137). Then, he should not forget about the goodness of his grandmother.

"*Despite everything*, she has been good to us" (italics added).

If he were to visit her, he should remind himself of how good she had been to him and his family. That could be done only if he stands in defiance of "everything" that she had done to them—"despite everything." There are two opposing ideas which make the decision difficult. No one in the family could forget how she treated them. Hema, Renu, and Shivan had their own stories narrating her "terrible way" of treating. Nevertheless, she had opened her house to them and let them stay. Shivan terms it as "hospitality."

But was it hospitality?

It is difficult to say. Yet, one could say it with difficulty—hospitality with difficulty. It was *difficult* hospitality. Anyway, if there is hospitality, that would only be difficult. There is no easy hospitality. It is never easy (Derrida 2000, 75–155; Caputo 1996).

Grandmother opened the house for them only after seeing Shivan. Though Hema had gone to her asking permission to stay in the house with her two children, she had denied it. She was ready to provide them with an allowance but not the space in her house (Selvadurai 2013, 22). It was Rosalind, the ayah, who thought, "let her see him." Seeing the "poor little boy" with "frightened glances," grandmother's mind changed. To her, he was "LIKE RAIN SOAKING A PARCHED LAND" (Ibid, 26). Thus, she opened her house for him, therefore, for the other two as well—mother and the sister, Renu. Yet, she continued to be obdurate towards her daughter and refused to have meals together with them.

Hema and Renu were aware that it was only because of Shivan that they got the chance to stay in the house. He was "the most important," and Renu wanted him to be "nice to Aachi." That niceness of Shivan would stop her from throwing them into the street. Hence, Shivan should be "nice" to his grandmother. Accordingly, he had to do different things, including going to Petah with his Aachi. He could not say "no" to her requests. There was no space for that. He feared the dire consequences of badly behaving with Aachi. She would throw them out. She is capable of that.

But was he *actually* afraid of that punishment?

He was aware that it was the maximum step that the grandmother could take against them. It was the limit of her power. On the other hand, he also knew the strength of his mother in managing such crucial situations. Therefore, it was not necessary that he feared Aachi and followed her commands in order to please her.

Nonetheless, it was not the *only* possibility. Each possibility is with another possibility.

Accordingly, there was another decisive one, and it was Renu's warning. She had threatened him in case of such eviction: "If that happens, I will always hate you" (Ibid). He feared the future hate of his sister. The future of hate was unbearable to him. It would be similar to the one in the story of "The Demoness Kali" narrated to him by his grandmother. Hence, fearing the sister capable of hate, he often tried following everyone's advice and pleasing Aachi to manage the space in her house, which is *her* space. Thus, by attempting to manage the space in her house, what he gained was nothing but hate of his sister and future filled with her hate.

Even if that space was for Shivan, and therefore for his family; it (space) was probably the only thing he did not have in that house. Space was given to him. The *given* always comes with some conditions. Consequently, he should show extreme obedience and loyalty to his grandmother. It is only then he could please her and win her heart. Her happiness is a prerequisite to their survival in the house. On the other hand, he could not please her in his way but in her way. But, how would he, "a little boy," understand the complexity of pleasing another?

Aachi was desperate for his love and respect. Until then, nobody, including her daughter, had loved or respected her. Though it might not be the case, at least, that is how she had felt. She accepted her life, deprived of love and respect, as a curse of some bad *karma* that she must have committed in the previous life. Since it is *karma*, she is unable to undo it. She should accept it and bear it. In so doing, she would pay it off. Apart from that, she should also collect merits by doing good *karma* during this life. It is only then she could hope for a better life in the coming birth. Thus, she believed in the idea of *karma* preached by Buddha. At the same time, she had twisted the same with her version and had come up with a different idea of *karma*, which she confidently appropriated to the one preached by Buddha. Accordingly, she had started constructing a *banamaduwa* (a hall in a temple where many people could sit and listen to the sermons of Buddhist monks), thinking that it would be enough merit for a good birth (Ibid, 218). It was her long-term goal. However, she also visited a Hindu temple every day for the evening *pooja*, seeking the intervention of Hindu gods in life's daily problems.

Worshipping Hindu Gods alongside Buddha is a part of Sinhala Buddhist society and culture (Gombrich and Obeyesekere 1988). Moreover, among these gods, Vishnu is very significant (Holt 2004) since, according to the *Mahavamsa*, he has been entrusted to survive Buddhism in Sri Lanka (Gombrich and Obeyesekere 1988, 18). However, there have been several attempts of Sinhala Buddhist monks, some Sinhala Buddhist national heroes, and political parties trying to stop Sinhala Buddhists worshipping Hindu gods. According to them, Buddhists should not believe in gods. If one does, he or she cannot be a Buddhist because belief in gods has got nothing to do with Buddhism (Ibid).

Worshipping gods and idols is central to Hinduism. If so, from where did the Sinhala Buddhist pick up this practice? Obeysekere and Gombrich associate it with cosmology. According to them, every society whichever adopted Buddhism has associated with a rich and complex cosmology.

> The cosmologies of all traditional societies tend to equate the natural order with the social order and both with the moral order; and probably none have done so more thoroughly than that of classical India, in its Hindu, Buddhist, and Jain variants. Sinhala Buddhism has inherited that classical Indian cosmology and added only minor local modifications.
>
> (Ibid, 17)

Now, this is an important point. On the one side, there is the *Teravada* Buddhist tradition. On the other side, there is the "Traditional Sinhala Buddhism" that entails certain practices, beliefs, and rituals connected to Indian cosmology. Obeyesekere and Gombrich project this influence to be a cosmological one (Ibid, 18).

Further, *Mahavamsa*'s claim of Buddha entrusting Buddhism to the hands of a god is highly paradoxical. It is contradictory to his *dhamma* emphasizing on change or transience as the only truth of everything: "*uppada, tithi, bhanga*" (which means something coming to exist, its existence, and its destruction or death). If that is the truth, his *dhamma* (teachings) itself is not an exception. It, too, is subjected to change. It had already started happening when he was alive; it continues to happen. On the other hand, Buddha considered *dhamma* to be *the* most powerful. Hence, no one has to protect it. Instead, *dhamma* protects everyone who follows it— "*dhammo have rakkathi dhammachari.*" Therefore, it is unlikely Buddha appointed anyone—be it Sakra, Vishnu, Sinhalese, Sri Lankans, etc.—to protect *dhamma* after his death. Nevertheless, this *entrusting job* said to be done by Buddha at his death bed contradicts the Buddhist philosophy. If we believe the popular reading of the chronicle, we also have to subscribe to this contradiction. And, I wonder whether Sri Lankan Sinhala Buddhists would be comfortable with doing such a thing!

Then, if one is a real Buddhist, if such a thing is possible, he or she should follow only the *dhamma* (*dharma*). There cannot be any other connection, including the one with cosmology. It is only such absoluteness that could grant a discourse of *pure* Buddhism. Nevertheless, what could be seen in the Sri Lankan Buddhist context is the opposite. Those who claim to be Sinhala Buddhists continue the practice of worshipping gods. They, like Shivan's grandmother, believe that gods could help them and protect them from danger and evil.

This fact highlights the impossibility of a *pure* Sinhala Buddhism and a *pure* Sinhala Buddhist society in Sri Lanka. It is already influenced by Hinduism. The presence of certain Hindu elements dismantles the hypothetical purity of Sinhala Buddhism practised in Sri Lanka. The impossible purity of Sinhala Buddhism due to its mixture with Hinduism challenges not only the sovereign space of Sinhala Buddhism but also the sovereignty of the Sri Lankan Sinhala Buddhist nation.

Shivan's grandmother was thus handling two things at the same time. On the one hand, she is to tackle her *karma*. On the other hand, she should please gods, especially Lord Ganesh by doing *poojas*. Despite many other errands undertaken to earn money, she had dedicated herself to these two different tasks. Meanwhile, Shivan came into her life, and she loved him. He was her happiness after a long time. She loved that happiness because she loved to be happy. That happiness came to her via Shivan. As she loved to be happy and loved the happiness that she felt because of Shivan, she loved Shivan. Love is always self-love. It is impossible to think of love without self-love. Yet, it becomes problematic when one wants to own the other out of love; when one wants to possess the other as if he/she is some property. Aachi had owned many properties around Colombo, and she had rented them out to different families. In the process, she felt even the tenants were her property. Somewhere, she seemed to have forgotten the difference between properties (objects) and people. Claim for the ownership had become her habit, and no one could change her. Not even Buddha and Ganesh. If possible, she could have tried to own these two as well. However, that was all about her properties, workers, and tenants with whom she did not feel emotionally attached. She was attached to them for money. In the case of Shivan, things were different. She was attached to him emotionally. By trying to convince Shivan with the benevolence of a grandmother, she had thought that she could gain control over him and possess him forever. Accordingly, she went on doing things for the happiness and the betterment of Shivan. In return, she expected love and respect from him through his obedience to follow her orders, to accept her requests, and to behave accordingly.

One could love the other. Yet, one cannot expect the other's love in return. That is impossible. When it is already an impossibility, how could one think or expect that the other would love *me* how *I* want him/her to do? But, when in love, this is what everyone thinks and expects from the other. It is a common thought to love—expectation. There is no love without this expectation. In love, one could only expect, yet with no guarantee.

So, she also expected that Shivan would love her according to her way.

Shivan loved her in *his* way, which was then a way of a child—childish. More than the love for her, he loved gifts that he received from her. On the other hand, he was afraid of her fury and its consequences. Moreover, he was also not sure whether he should love her at all. This dilemma was partly due to his own experiences with her, which were not pleasant. They were rather torturous, and he "hated" those afternoons spent with her after school. Till he became 13 years old, he used to keep "vigil" in the grandmother's room while she slept. Consequently, he could not play with his sister. After that, he was to accompany her for the works related to her properties and to sit with Sunil Mama during his weekly visits to her to clear out problems in the legal documents. Apart from those, he also saw the fights between his mother and his grandmother. Those verbal arguments were ugly, and their years-old rivalry often exploded in a manner that they ended up cursing each other for having to bear the other. One such moment erupted on the day when the mother found the grandmother beating Shivan for his mistake. She was furious. Though Rosalind tried to calm her down, it was fruitless.

> "that wretched witch," my mother whispered. She strode out of the room [...]

> When she got to my grandmother's doorway, she ripped back the curtain and went in. "How dare you touch my child!"
>
> My grandmother was getting dressed for temple. "Get out of my room."
>
> "You will not ruin my children's life like you did mine."
>
> [...]
>
> "Remember your place. This is my house. I have allowed you to stay. You are lucky."
>
> "You allow me to stay because you don't want to lose face with your friends and our relatives."
>
> "You are wrong. I let you stay because I shudder to think what disgrace you would bring on our family name if I allowed you to live on your own. What horrible mistakes you would make."
>
> "I don't know what you mean." My mother crossed her arms over her chest.
>
> My grandmother let out a bark of a laugh. She leaned towards my mother.
>
> "Look at where your mistakes have brought your children. Look at them! Tamil, poor and undereducated! You're a disgraceful mother. A failure!"
>
> (Selvadurai 2013, 30–31)

That was the first time Shivan saw his mother and grandmother quarrelling with each other. Mother's eyes were filled with tears. What unfolded during the quarrel is bitter than the quarrelling itself. From one side, it was the anger of the mother towards her mother for destroying her life by not letting her pursue higher education as her will. She had wanted to enter university. It was her dream. However, she could not decide from which stream she should try the university entrance. It was her mother who had decided that she should do sciences. Objection was useless (Ibid, 48). Accordingly, she was to study physics, chemistry, zoology, and botany, and she did not enjoy it. Yet, her mother had arranged afterschool classes for her by bringing tutors into the house. One day, when she came home late missing her classes, her mother had dragged her by the hair to her bedroom, slapped her all the way, locked her inside the room, and pocketed the key with her. "Let her starve in there tonight" (Ibid, 49).

Hema did not like her mother, Daya, because she never felt the warmth of the mother. Her words were "few" and "stiff." They were said in a "distant but pleasant tone" as if she was not her daughter but a child of a servant or of a cousin. Moreover, she too was "grateful for this lack of interest." She did not want her love. Instead, she received all the love from Rosalind (Ibid, 44). She had lost her kind father when she was a child of eight years. By the age of 15, she was frustrated with her mother. She had thought university life would bring her the desired freedom. The incident of severe punishment had broken her within, and she only wanted to "escape." Yet, she could not tell it. Though she had sensed already what she would do, "it was so awful that she turned from it," not knowing where her actions would leave her. Therefore, she tried her best to study for the exam. She worked very well. But, when she went for the exam, she could not write it. Instead of writing the exam, she found herself observing "a gecko crawling after a fly on the ceiling, the spinning, humming fans, the girls crouched over their desks, the invigilators standing in the doorways and murmuring to each other across the hall." When she realized that too much time had passed, she had started answering the questions "fanatically." For four days of the exam, things went like this. Despite her attempt to focus on the questions, her mind "drifted" from them. After some time, an inner voice within her would cry, "What are you doing! You are eating yourself!" (Ibid, 50–51).

When the results came, she found her friends less intelligent than her entering university. On the other hand, she saw her mother trembling after seeing the unexpected results: "Oh, God, I am cursed. [...] My happiness denied. The naked peréthi, I *am* the naked peréthi" (Ibid, 52).

It was then she angrily revealed some truth she had managed to gather against her dominating mother. "Don't worry, I will never end up like you. Because I am not some *vesi* who throws herself at a man and ruts around with him on a beach, like a bitch in heat" (Ibid).

Daya was shocked to hear this from her daughter. She stared at her "in disbelief." For a week, she stayed in her darkened room. After that, one evening, she had got up with some great energy, wore a white sari, and went for evening *pooja* at the nearby temple. It was the beginning of her "religiosity." Meanwhile, caught in the agony of a lost dream and having to live with a mother who "never spoke to her," Hema hated her home. Often in the middle of the night, she moaned aloud. It was, then, when she was "desperate for affection," she had met her husband. Daya did not like this "foolish" choice of her daughter: "A Tamil and a Christian." Yet, Hema held onto her choice and got married to him (Ibid, 53).

Hema's anger did not go away. It only aggravated with the life she had to bear with her husband. Escalating tension between the Tamil and the Sinhalese during the 1970s had made him feel uneasy at his work place. He was resented by all the other Sinhala waiters and workers in the guest house. They called him "Tamil dog." However, he liked spending his whole day there in the office "to avoid" his wife. One day, while doing the accounts sitting in his office, he died of a heart attack. Finally, she had to return to her mother's house as a widow with two children.

Despite her disdain towards her daughter, Daya, after seeing the little boy, let them stay at her house. But, she did not come to have meals sitting together with her. Hema had to have her meal on the back verandah. That was the punishment given to her on the day she had spoken against her mother. Though years had passed since then, things did not seem to have changed from Daya's side. She continued to be the rude mother or the rude woman despite her dedication to some religiosity and love for Shivan.

Till the quarrel broke, no one was aware why Daya had let Hema and her children stay at her house. All of them, including Rosalind, had thought that it was only because of Shivan that she had opened her house for them. But, what is revealed during the squabble is different. She had done it only because she was concerned about her "family name." It is to protect the name and the dignity of the family that she had let them stay.

Then, how could it be considered hospitality?

She reminds her daughter about the place where she is. "Remember *your* place. This is *my* house. I have *allowed* you to stay" (italics added).

She had to remind her daughter Hema of it because Hema behaved *as if* she had forgotten it. She cannot afford to forget it. If she does or if it happens, she has to be reminded of her forgetfulness which had made her forget that she should not forget her "place." It is a place in someone else's place; therefore, it is not *her* place; it can never be hers. It is *given* to her. It is possible for someone to feel a sense of belonging when it comes to certain people and places. It is so because of the familiarity determined by the duration of stay or the contact. But, familiarity does not exhaust the foreignness or the strangeness. She is a guest. A guest is, as Derrida would say, "first of all a foreigner" (2000, 73). It is the foreigner who receives the hospitality of the host because hospitality is due for the foreigner. By appearing in front of her mother's house after becoming a widow, Hema had stood for her "right to hospitality." It is this right "what makes hospitality possible, or the hospitable relationship to the foreigner possible" (Ibid, 23–25). And her mother grants it by *letting* her enter the house. She gives some space to them from her space. If she wanted, she could have refuted it because it is *her* house. Moreover, she is the head of the house. Therefore, she has the power to decide—sovereignty. Discussing the "foreigner question" Derrida explains the collusion between sovereignty and hospitality as follows:

> No hospitality, in the classic sense, without sovereignty of oneself over one's home, but since there is also no hospitality without finitude, sovereignty can be only exercised by filtering, choosing, and thus by excluding and doing violence.
>
> (Ibid, 55)

Thus, the master of the house has the power of hospitality, and the guest should not behave in an encroaching manner while making his/her space there. In case of such behaviour, the host ends up becoming "hostage" of the guest. In that sense, hospitality is a risky affair since the guest could become a "hostile subject"—enemy (Ibid). However, in case of a violation, the host would take the necessary measures to privatize and secure the space.

Ever since Hema entered the house with her two children, her mother often stayed in her room. It was where she felt secure. Entering the room with anger, Hema intimidated the mother asking, "how dare you touch my child?" (italics added). Hema seems to be saying that her mother does not have a right to touch her child. She should not dare to do such a thing. She had crossed her limits and hit the child with a slipper. So, she rushes to her mother's room ripping back the curtain *as if* to remind her of *her* limits. While trying to remind her of *her* limits, she actually ended up crossing the limits. She has already violated her limits by crossing the doorstep to her mother's room while pulling out the curtain. Curtain, which marks the entry to her mother's room, is not only the one that gives her privacy but also that which bears the difference between host and the guest—threshold. Therefore, it stands as the possible place of violence where the guest could violate the norms and ethos of the home, which is that of the host. Hence, by ripping it back, Hema has violated the order of her mother's house—the law of hospitality. It is the hostility of the guest that makes the host shout, "Get out of my room." She tells her the basis for offering this hospitality—"Family name." In fact, it is not only the base of this particular hospitality from Daya to Hema but also the condition of hospitality in general—the "conditional hospitality" (Ibid, 21–26). Then, this favour, which she had offered to Hema, could also be offered to anyone in general "as a family." But, here, there is something more to this guest who has got a *family with her*. This phrase is ambiguous here. On the one hand, Hema is not the absolute other. She is coming from a family. She has got a name by which she could be addressed or called out "as a family." On the other hand, she is also carrying her family with her by accompanying her two children. However, the family name of the guest is not only a name enabling her addressed "as a family" but also the name of the host family. It is the same family name shared by the host and the guest. They both *bear* the same family. They both have been doing that ever since they became the mother and the daughter of the same family—bearing each other being in the same family; bearing each other for the sake of the family; bearing each other in the name of the family. So much bearing just to prevent the "disgrace" coming to the "family name." But, it is already a family name with some "disgrace." Hema had managed to gather some story of disgrace about her mother from her other relatives. It was a story, which made her mother a "*vesi*" in front of everyone in the family, also in the village; finally, it reached her daughter's ears. Thus, she did not have a defence. It damaged her character, as well as her name, which was also her family name. Here, when I say family, it is not only the family that she was born to but also the family that both the mother and the daughter share, being *women*. The latter is a family name known for "disgrace." There have been many stories that talk about the disgrace of the family of women. It is well known just not to the ones in a particular locality but to everyone in the world. Disgrace attached to women is a historical one. There is a history of women which projects women as disgraceful

(Cixous 1976, 875–893, 2005). It is, in fact, a projection of phallocentric projects. Those projects managed to project disgrace as a trait of a woman family. Daya could not erase it or undo it by narrating her story, which is different from the ones told about her by others. No one was ready to listen to a different version of the same story. No version could challenge the dominant and popular one. After all, it is also the version of the religion that she followed. There is a book, which narrates stories about Buddha's previous births—*Pansiya Panas Jathakaya*. They all explain the effect of *karma*. Among those stories, there are also those about women. Most of those stories narrate how disgraceful women could be in addressing their carnal appetite.

Considering all the *jathaka* tales in the book, they are narrations about the Buddha attaining the Buddhahood. However, these narrations have been crucial, for they influence on shaping the cognition of Sri Lankan Sinhala Buddhist society. In the process, people took those narrations to be the ultimate truth about certain things. It is a dangerous take. Accordingly, things told about women in the stories became decisive in understanding women in general (Menike 2016, 154). Those stories, known as the narrations by Buddha to his disciples, became the greatest source of truth and knowledge about women. Meanwhile, people, (un)consciously though, referred to Buddha as the source of that knowledge. Hence, disgrace is one such truth about women. It is their nature—intrinsic. Those stories are repeatedly narrated to Sinhala Buddhists by Buddhist monks and some laity during especial religious programmes held in temples during *poya* days or in individual houses. As well as some of the stories are included in text books as a part of the school syllabus. Apart from that, they are also bedtime stories or leisure-time stories narrated to children by their elders (Ibid, 154 – 155). Stories about the ghosts narrated by Shivan in *The Hungry Ghosts* are the ones narrated to him by his mother and his grandmother. Nevertheless, whenever the stories are narrated, it is not the same story, but the same different story. There is a difference in each telling. It is the telling that brings differences to stories. In such a context, is it possible to have a direct reference?

Anyway, considering the disgrace attached to the family name—women/female, every woman could be a disgrace to her family, clan, community, and so on. No sociocultural, economic, and political movement, which took place in Sri Lanka or anywhere in the world in the name of liberating women, could change this deep-rooted idea on women. Women are disgraced. They are to live in disgrace, with disgrace.

Daya has been living with that disgrace; she bore it silently—silent bearer. She is not only a silent bearer of disgrace but also of *her* story. She never got the space to tell her story. No one had given that space to her by lending an ear. It remained unarticulated. She thus lived a guilty life with an unarticulated story, and that knowledge "corroded" her (Selvadurai 2013, 259).

Nonetheless, she learnt to accept it as her *karma*. It is the most euphemistic way to look at it. Though it does not solve the matter, it would, at least, help in lessening the violence. Buddha had not explained the idea of *karma* as a solution to any problem. It does not ask anyone to worry about the actions done in the past. Rather, it asks one to realize the mistakes committed and their effect on others, and, then, learn from those lessons and be self-responsible for the actions done in the present. Thus, the Buddhist concept of *karma* demands a strong sense of self-responsibility. Accordingly, one should not desire the self or happiness of the self at the cost of the other. It necessitates one to be de-attached from the self. Moreover, everyone should undertake this self-responsibility as an everyday practice.[4]

In Daya's troubled world, she had settled down with a poor idea of *karma*. Accordingly, she had convinced herself with the idea, many unfortunate conditions in her life are due to some bad *karma* in the previous birth, though almost all of them were the consequences of her actions or *karma* in the present life. It appeared even more ridiculous[5] when she justified *her* violence on others as the effect of their (own) bad karma in *their* previous birth. Accordingly, they were to undergo her violence in the present life. Moreover, she also thought that those who were under her hand were still lucky to have a "fair" person like her. That luck is also probably because, as per her version of *karma*, they had done some good *karma* too. This is not only Daya's version of *karma* but also that of many Sinhala Buddhists. It is the popular version in society, and some Sinhala Buddhist monks also legitimize the same. However, this version of *karma*, like a poor translation, differs from the one that Buddha said to have preached. But every version of *karma*, which refers to the Buddhist idea of *karma*, differs from the same. This difference is unavoidable. Every translation is gained with a loss (Derrida 1985, 93–161, 2002a, 105–134; Benjamin 1999). Therefore, there is no perfect or complete translation. Yet, it should try to be as close as possible to the source text. The one that appears to be closer to the source text is seen as a good translation, which is also, on the other hand, as Derrida would say elsewhere, "the least bad." Then, Daya's version of *karma*, which is also the popular one in society, is a very poor translation of Buddha's idea of *karma*. It is of very poor quality, for it has damaged what is *fundamental* to Buddha's idea of *karma*—self-responsibility in violence. No Buddhist version of *karma* can afford to lose the idea of self-responsibility. The concept of *karma* is all time relevant and valid only because of its emphasis on self-responsibility.

However, the version of *karma* popular in Sri Lankan Sinhala Buddhist society, especially since independence to date, seems to have missed it—the sense of self-responsibility—in the process of socio, cultural, political, economic, and linguistic translation. It does not mean that it has absolutely lost it. That does not happen so because that *cannot* happen. It does have the idea of responsibility, yet it is not *self*-responsibility. Therefore, it could be anybody's responsibility. It could be passed onto anyone. As it is thus passable, everyone could get rid of the burden of bearing it by passing it to the other. Therefore, it is more of (an)other's responsibility rather than mine. Daya always had passed her responsibility to others. She was never prepared to bear it. She was like those Sinhala Buddhist governments in post-independent Sri Lanka, which always enjoyed passing the responsibility of their violent actions to others.

Daya never felt that she was responsible for Hema's miserable life. She always thought she had accomplished her responsibility as a mother, for she fed her daughter, spent money on her education, and gave new clothes and some other gifts. She was often ready to give some financial allowance to her because, for her, money is the most important thing that one could give to the other. According to her, Hema was solely responsible for her misery. She could not help it. Hema had understood that her mother would never take such a responsibility. She never knew about self-responsibility. That is why Hema sees her mother's hospitality as mere manipulation.

However, after the quarrel between the mother and the grandmother, it was difficult for Shivan to love his grandmother. Yet, he had to manage and settle down with something which appeared like obedience-cum-love. It became further vague when he began to feel grandmother's gifts to him like a "betrayal" of his mother, "an affront to her poverty" (Selvadurai 2013, 37). On the one hand, being a child, he was attracted to gifts. On the other hand, having to support his poor family by adjusting with grandmother's un-kind nature without betraying his mother, it became difficult and complex for him to receive gifts from the grandmother. At times, as Paranjape (2013) writes, receiving is more difficult than giving. It is so because one has to give so much to receive in the sense that one should go out of his/her way to receive what is given. Receiving is thus not the opposite of giving; rather, it is another way of giving (Menike 2020). Shivan could not resist receiving; he did not have a choice in receiving. If he did, he would have received only what he wanted to receive from his grandmother, which is the permission for them to stay at her house. But, that option was not there for him. It was imperative for him to receive everything given to him by her for him to receive the only thing that he had wanted. Thus, his relationship with Aachi is a complex one, and he could never be genuine with her.

However, he was genuinely aware of his in-genuineness towards Aachi, and he continued to feel guilty for the same. Moreover, he was not sure whether such genuineness would mean anything to her. She never appeared to be appreciative of such morality. The more he realized her cruel, inconsiderate, and exploitative nature, the more he justified his own ingenuine behaviour with her. He continued to lie to her even after he went to Canada. Though he and his family left for Canada in search of freedom not only from the discrimination and suppression that they had to undergo being Tamils but also from the pressure from their grandmother, they had to depend on her to survive there. As well as, Aachi too could not cut all ties with them after coming to know their plan to move to Canada. She was sure that it was her daughter's decision, and she cursed her for that, though it was Shivan who had taken the decision.

She never doubted Shivan but his mother. She was blinded, on the one side, by her hate towards her daughter; on the other side, by her love towards Shivan. She never saw one with the other. It was impossible for her to see that she *did not* see. She did not see that she did not see. Accordingly, she saw Hema as an enemy, a bad karmic effect—"wild bitch of a daughter" (Selvadurai 2013, 72) who would do only the things which go against or hurt her mother. Therefore, in her eyes, Hema was guilty not only for *her* words, gestures, or actions but also for those of others. When driven by hate, one always tends to suspect the other. The other becomes the source of evil, harm, and malevolence. But, it is quite the opposite when one loves the other. In love, one hesitates to suspect the other; one does not think that the loved other could hate the one who loves. It is so, not because one believes the other and other's love; rather, it is because one believes in one's love for the other. Certainly, one should believe in his/her love and be confident with it in the sense that he/she should be able to tell his/her self that *Yes, I love him/her. I do not doubt myself in this love that I feel for the other. I have no doubts about my love for the other. I love the other undoubtedly*. This self-affirmation is necessary to love the other. In fact, Michael wants Shivan to check with himself whether he could hold such self-affirmation regarding his love for Michael. He says, "Shivan, if you love me ..."

One could affirm one's love for the other only by affirming it to the self. And, this affirmation could be possible only by questioning the self. In love, one should take one's (own) self into confidence regarding his/her love for the other. It is only then one could be self-confident in its love. This, in turn, says that one could love the other *only if* one is self-confident about his/her love. If it is not, one should not say *I love you* to (an)other—morality. That is why the idea of morality or ethics is fundamental to the question of love. If one is unable to affirm it to the self, it is better, as Paranjape would suggest in *Body Offering* (2013), not to express it to the other despite consequences. Let alone the expression or expressing love, he is afraid even to mention the word itself; to take it as a word to play with and to manipulate the situations in order to address one's desires. It is not a word or a name that could be used to name a play of bodies.

However, here, self-confidence in love does not mean overconfidence. One should not be overconfident about one's love for the other in a manner that one begins to decide *for* the other. One cannot be confident about its love to be the other's love or love of the other. In other words, one cannot appropriate one's love with that of the other. Such an attempt is unethical. But, one cannot love the other without trying to appropriate the other (DeArmitt 2014). (This idea will be discussed in detail in the coming chapters). In the case of Aachi, she thinks that she has loved her grandson satisfactorily. She has never denied anything that he had asked for him. In fact, she had given many things to him even before he asked for them. Since all his needs are entertained, she was sure that there would not be any reason for Shivan to think bad about her or to hurt her. She was confident that Shivan loved her love and wanted only *that* love and *that* way of loving. Thus, she was blinded by her (own) love for him and failed to see her (own) blindness, which prevented her from seeing Shivan as (an)other—another one different from the one that she thinks and expects him *to be*. It is this blindness, which makes her believe that Shivan had nothing to do with the plan for Canada (Selvadurai 2013, 73).

In the unbearable pain of losing the last thing she loved in her life, she desperately attempted to hold him close to her by getting him a house in Canada. Though Hema said "no" to this offer, she insisted on it, saying, "This house is for Shivan" (Ibid, 74). Nevertheless, as Hema's low financial condition could not facilitate them with a house in Canada, they wondered whether they could reject the grandmother's offer. If they accept her offer, they are bound to bear her, tolerate her, even if they do not want to do so—indigestible truth. When they stayed in her house, they lived this difficult truth hoping someday they would be free from her. Now, when the moment of freedom has come to them for them to be free from her house, her presence, and her dominance, they are unable to execute it. It looks *as if* they are destined to live a harsh truth.

But are they the only ones facing this destiny?

It is everybody's destiny of/in living—life. Life is a harsh truth *to live*. One could neither have it nor could one leave it. One could only struggle in between these two extremes. If one wants to have it, one has to have it fully because, in having, one has only two options: *either* to have *or* not to have. On the other hand, if one wants to leave it, one has to leave it fully because, in leaving, one could *either* leave *or* not leave. Semantically, these two verbs are very conditioning. However, in this struggle, everything is a struggle and one *has to* struggle—the condition. Accordingly, the desired freedom is also a part of that struggle while being a struggle itself. Freedom is a struggle, and it could be *only* a struggle—infinity. One could never have it achieved fully. One could only try to achieve it. Freedom is only *to achieve*.

Hence, Shivan and his family are *to achieve* freedom in Canada. This journey in pursuit of freedom is not comfortable. It becomes further complex when another condition is added to the struggle—freedom in a foreign land. People in the countries from South Asia often assume that life in Canada, the USA, Australia, and Europe is better than the one that they have in their region. They tend to believe that those countries could offer better lives to their citizens in terms of freedom and happiness. Moreover, newspapers, magazines, movies, and television programmes especially produced, distributed, and transmitted in the region often appear to strengthen and confirm this assumption. It appears that their job is nothing but to affirm assumptions. But, in a way, there are only assumptions *to affirm*. On the other hand, Hollywood, too, has its share in this project of projecting some freedom *already* available in the West. West or Europe appears as the space of ultimate freedom, especially to those who are outside it. Hence, people who remain *outside* often desire to enter there and be like one of them. At times, some even tend to be like *any* of them to become one of them.

By the age of 17, Shivan, a voracious reader, too, got acquainted with many such printed materials, ranging from the works by Georgette Heyer, Victoria Holt, Dickens, Thackeray, Austen, Agatha Christie, P.G. Wodehouse, Leon Uris, and Tolstoy to the biographies of old Hollywood stars (Ibid, 55). He read about the torrid sex lives, the ghastly childhoods, the ruinous marriages, the alcoholism, and drug abuse, the sheer madness of the likes of Joan Crawford, Viven Leigh, Judy Garland, and Jean Harlow as if they were spicy potboilers., and devoured practically anything (Ibid). One of his favourites was the biography of Montgomery Clift. While reading it, he stumbled onto a word, which he had not encountered before— "homosexuality" (Ibid). (And, later it was no more a word which he had read in another's biography, but a word without which he could not speak about his life—*The Hungry Ghosts.*) Further, he also could hear things about America, a place most of them had "chosen" for "higher education," often spoken by boys in his school. According to them, besides offering a "superior education," America was also "a Mecca for sexual adventure" (Ibid, 56). After becoming a member of the American Center Library, he could access periodicals and prospectuses for American universities along with copies of SAT and TOFEL study books. He was attracted by the pictures of students lying in the grass, sun glinting in their hair, or hunched around a cafeteria table in earnest talk, or walking arm in arm down a corridor in those prospectuses and imagined himself being there. He thought that he would be able to become the person that he really knew himself to be: "popular," "gregarious," "witty," and "handsome" (Ibid, 57). However, with the news of Canadian and Australian embassies offering fast-track immigration to Tamils due to the escalating upheavals in the country, he became "desperate" and cycled to the Canadian High Commission in Colombo to get an immigration form (Ibid, 67). Meanwhile, Hema thought that her daughter, Renu could go to a "better university" which is not "constantly shutting down because of student hartals" (Ibid, 69). Though Renu hesitated about the idea of going to Canada due to her already started university life, after listening to Sriyani Karunaratne, her history professor, she too agreed to go. Her professor had told her that there were programmes on feminism in the West called "women studies" and she could pursue her interest with greater focus (Ibid).

Three of them, like many other Sri Lankans, had imagined the world in the West to be the best world and desired to begin a new life there. However, Aachi was worried about her grandson, and she wanted to help him to build his life in a "foreign land"—the land of their freedom. They were going to be foreigners in some other land, despite their right to hospitality. The right is possible only if there is a house to receive them and accommodate them. As every hospitality is conditional hospitality, guests are also liable to expulsion. Considering all these, she decided to buy a house in Canada for Shivan so that they have a house of their own. Accordingly, after a week spent in Bhavan's house in Canada, they managed to buy a tiny row house in Scarborough for themselves. It was their first house in Canada.

This unforgettable "hospitality" of his grandmother became decisive to his visit to Sri Lanka. A few years of life in Canada had irked him. In fact, it had tired all of them out. What Canada could offer them was different from what they had expected from it. It could give only what it *could* afford to give—hospitality. They were to manage the rest, and each of them got busy with managing their lives. That is what everybody does everywhere—managing life under many different conditions. They could understand this truth only after they came to Canada. It appeared as if they had come from Sri Lanka to Canada only to realize this *truth*. Each of them regretted their decision which brought them to Canada. They are like the boy who went to *Araby* in the Joyce's (1914).

However, what is done cannot be undone. It is not only a line from Shakespeare's *Macbeth* but also the truth about the inability to reverse actions. This inability is universal. If it differs, it is only in language. Every language has its way of expressing it. Shivan remembers how it is being said in Sinhala, using two words for rice: "*haal*" and "*buth*." The first one is for the hardened grain. The second is for what the grain becomes when it is boiled. He says, "in speaking of our inability to reverse actions, our inability to change karma's ripening, we say that *haal*, once it has started to become buth, cannot revert to being haal" (Ibid, 131).

Hence, they could not go back to Sri Lanka, though Canada had become a "shit of a country."

Falling in Love: Violence and Violation

Michael's request for truth is a question not only about love but also about violence. It concerns some violence done by Shivan by violating the condition of love—truth. Truth is necessary *to love*. One cannot love another without being true to one's self and his/her love for the other. If one does so, it cannot be *true* love. Hence, Shivan has already hurt Michael. But is he the only one hurt here? What about Shivan? Isn't he hurt because of the question posed by Michael? Isn't Michael violent by making this request after two years of relationship?

Two years had passed between them, and they stayed happily for two years. Shivan had always wanted to make Michael happy with his love, care, concern, and jokes. Nevertheless, despite all these, Shivan still dreamt of Mili. He would run into him on the street in Vancouver or Toronto

(Ibid, 315). Their conversations in the dreams were friendly but stilted in that way of school friends who had lost touch. Whenever he woke up, he woke up to his "old restlessness," which made his day uneasy to the extent that he was even "irritated by Michael's presence." Due to some habits of Michael he felt Michael was "less than Mili." Though he was "aware" of how "unfair" the comparison is, he could not help it. Feeling "guilty" and helpless made him a difficult lover in a way that they started quarrelling with each other, though they went through the "rituals and tasks that bonded" them. Eventually, both of them managed to capitulate and renew a "sweetness flooded" life. Yet, he felt the presence of some "invisible residue." The realization that Michael would not "withstand the entry" of his past into their life made him tense (Ibid, 315–316).

However, with the arrival of his mother and sister in the Vancouver apartment, things only got worse within Shivan. It was not only because of the dreams and their effect on his everyday life with Michael but also his mother's question, which reminded him of his responsibility to Michael. One should not try to escape from responsibility, and Shivan, too, knew it. He felt "guilty" for not being responsible in the way he should be. In spite of this realization, he could not be brave to improve his condition, for he feared the consequences of being responsible. One does not fear so much to *do* things because it is easy *to do* or *to act* but the consequences. Consequences could influence the present condition either for better or for worse. And, no one wants anything to go from bad to worse. Therefore, if not for good, one at least tries to remain in the present condition preventing further falls. Bad is always a better degree than the worse. Shivan has been trying to maintain the present condition of life with quarrels and arguments. It seems that some amount of quarrelling and certain types of quarrels are possible, allowed, or entertained within a relationship. They could easily pass as "normal" or "usual." After all, as Blanchot would say in *The Idyll*, quarrels are "usual" between young married people (1999, 19). Though both quarrelling and quarrels are violent, when such unpleasant things happen between lovers or partners, some tend to term them *love-quarrels*—euphemism, though there is nothing to love about quarrels. No one quarrels in a lovely way. Moreover, one cannot love *to quarrel* though one could quarrel *to love*. Whoever, therefore, considers quarrels as normal, usual, unavoidable or, say, even, necessary, he/she indirectly subscribes, accepts, permits, or, in Marc Crépon's word, "consents" violence. Then, Shivan, too, had to adopt some violence in order to keep another kind of violence away from them—revelation. So doing, he had expected only the longevity of his relationship with Michael.

However, this effort of his could not make him non-violent. He has done violence to his beloved by hurting him by hiding things. He has failed to prevent the very thing that he had wanted to prevent—violence. In any case, did he have a better option other than the one he chose?

There were only two options left with him: either to reveal his past with Mili or to not reveal it. For some reason unknown to himself, he could not reveal it to Michael at the very outset of their relationship. It is not possible to start relationships by telling everything about one's self. On the other hand, one could be in a relationship only by telling things about the self to the other, by introducing the self to the other, and by addressing the other by telling things about the self. Thus, one begins *to tell*. But, in telling, one could only *begin* to tell, to say, to express without ever being able to complete it. One should go on telling in order to tell—infinity. There would always be something that could not be said, told, or expressed, which in turn would confirm, there is always something more *to say*. Shivan, too, has been telling things about himself to Michael. Consequently, Michael got familiar with the names of the people that Shivan has been talking about while talking about himself to Michael. Yet he had never heard of the name, Mili. It was the only name Shivan had not brought into the conversation. He *could not* (Selvadurai 2013, 340). This inability has been going on for two years. Now, could this weakness be reduced or defined as "lying"? Is it a lie? Has he lied to Michael by not talking about Mili? Who could be certain that it was a lie and Shivan has been a liar? How could one come to such a conclusion?

However, Shivan's silence regarding Mili cannot be absolved of violence.

But, what about Michael and his request?

Michael is not *not* violent. He too is violent by making the request. It is insisting, demanding, and commanding in a manner that the other has no way out but to respond—obligation, compulsion. It has already put the other in a difficult or uncomfortable condition. Was it necessary for him to ask for the truth after spending two years with Shivan? What good would it do *now*? Was not he convinced of Shivan's love? If he were not, how did he spend two years with him? By posing this question, has he not disturbed the continuity of their relationship?

The request is a blow to their relationship since it calls everything about their relationship into question. He feels the urge to question. It is irresistible because he needs to hear "the truth." This need for truth, on the other hand, puts the truth that he had heard for the last two years at risk, *as if* it is not the truth he had heard, *as if* what he heard is not true; *as if* it is not true what he heard. So doing, he not only doubts and questions Shivan but also his (own) self, his (own) ears, capacities, capabilities, and knowledge. He doubts what he heard. He is not sure whether he heard Shivan correctly, whether what he heard from Shivan is correct, or whether he could hear him at all. Then, it is not only about telling but also about hearing—hearing and being heard. Problematizing Sassurean circuit of communication, Derrida, in *Of Grammatology*, gives a great deal to the difference between the two (1994, 63). However, Michael could opt to hear the truth only by challenging the one already there. He is unable to continue with Shivan without questioning him. If he does not interrogate him, the doubt may continue in silence, and that would not do any good, for the silence does not assure peace and harmony. It is so, because silence too is violent (Derrida 1978, 97–192). Hence, he should ask this violent question to stop another kind of violence. There is no future to their relationship without this violence. The future of love and friendship is based on violence. Questioning, requesting, or arguing for clarifications is still better rather than making conclusions silently by appropriating and reducing the other into one's knowledge, language, and definition. Then, Michael's request-cum-question is, in fact, a "violent" or "non-ethical" opening of ethics (Derrida 1994, 139–140; 2002). His request brings a rupture to the relationship, disrupting its flow. And, that is what Shivan wanted to avoid happening. But no relationship could continue without ruptures, breaks, or discontinuities—finitude. Every relationship continues in discontinuities and never forms a complete whole. It is so due to the presence of the other—truth. No relationship could be guarded against this truth because it is *that*, which protects, secures, saves, and strengthens every relationship redeeming it and lifting it from a battle of power, where one tries to dominate the other. Relationships are not about control, domination, and subjugation where always one side ends up winning; nor are they about victory or success. Instead, they are about love, care, responsibility, and ethics, for which there should be no limit. Any genuine relationship of love, care, respect, and responsibility is possible only by contesting and overcoming the boundaries of self-desire for belongingness and ownership, which put limits *to love*, *to care*, and *to respect* the other. Now, such an effort *to overcome* the boundaries that guard the self against the other could be initiated only by breaking, undoing, and unmaking them with the *force* of love that loves the other. In such force of love, being is de-attached, distanced, and moved away from self, and, he/she is transferred, transformed, transcended, and metamorphosed him/her as (an)other being. Then, efforts of such kind need some violence. But this violence is ethical, for it is initiated to undo barriers that prevent self (being) loving the other. Therefore, Michael's request to hear the truth for love is both ethical and violent at the same time. If in love, such violence—disruption, interruption, and interrogation—is necessary *to love*.

Notes

1 Sasanka Perera, *The Ethnic Conflict in Sri Lanka: A Historical and Sociopolitical Outline* (Washington DC: World Bank, 2001), http://documents.wolrdbank.org/curated/en/727811468302711738; A. Jeyaratnam Wilson, *Sri Lankan Tamil Nationalism: Its Origins and Development in the Nineteenth and Twentieth Centuries* (Vancouver: UBC Press, 2000); Stanley Jeyaraja Tambiah, *Sri Lanka: Ethnic Fratricide and the Dismantling of Democracy* (Delhi: Oxford University Press, 1986); Laavanyan M. Ratnapalan, "Memories of Ethnic Violence in Sri Lanka Among Immigrant Tamils in the UK," in *Ethnic and Racial Studies* (UK: Routledge, 2011), http://hal.archives-ouvrtes.fr/hal-00713344; James Manor,

The Expedient Utopian: Bandaranaike and Ceylon (Cambridge: Cambridge University Press, 1989); Neil Devotta, "Control Democracy Institutional Decay, and the Quest for Eelam: Explaining Ethnic Conflict in Sri Lanka," *Pacific Affairs* 73, no. 1 (2000): 55–76; K.M. De Silva, *Reaping the Whirlwind: Ethnic Conflict, Ethnic Politics in Sri Lanka* (London: Penguin, 1998).

2 Rajan Hoole, *Sri Lanka: The Arrogance of Power: Myths, Decadence & Murder* (Jaffna: University Teachers for Human Rights, 2001); Laavanya M Ratnapalan, "Memories of Ethnic Violence in Sri Lanka Among Immigrant Tamils in the UK," in *Ethnic and Racial Studies* (UK: Routledge, 2011), https://hal.archives-ouvertes.fr/hal-00713344; Judith Betts and Claire Higgins, "The Sri Lankan Civil War and Australia's Migration Policy Response: A Historical Case Study with Contemporary Implications," *Asia & the Pacific Policy Studies* 4, no. 2 (2017), https://onlinelibrary.wiley.com/doi/full/10.1002/app5.181; Leonie Sadercock et al., "The Quest for an Inclusive City: An Exploration of Sri Lanka Tamil Experience of Integration in Toronto and Vancouver," in *Research on Immigration and Integration in the Metropolis* (RIIM): Working Paper Series (2004), https://www.yumpu.com/en/document/read/33358835/the-quest-for-an-inclusive-city-metropolis-bc.

3 See Nayomi Munaweera's *Island of A Thousand Mirrors* (Haryana: Hachette India Local, 2013); "Liberation Tigers of Tamil Eelam: Mapping Militant Organizations," accessed September, 08, 2021. http://web.stanford.edu/group/mappingmilitants/cgi-bin/groups/view/225; "Living in Fear: Child Soldiers and the Tamil Tigers in Sri Lanka," accessed September 08, 2021. http://www.hrw.org/report/2004/11/10/living-fear/child-soldiers-and-tamil-tigers-sri-lanka; "Four Sri Lankan Soldiers Convicted of Raping Tamil Women," accessed September 08, 2021. https://www.bbc.com/news/34470053.

4 Buddhism suggests five precepts to be followed by every human regularly. They are: to abstain from killing/murder, to abstain from stealing, to abstain from sensuous misconduct, to abstain from lying, and to abstain from intoxicating drinks and drugs.

5 B.R. Ambedkar in *Buddha and His Dhamma* (1957) and many other essays have critically dealt with the Buddhist idea of karma with regard to the socially discriminated people in India. For a better understanding in this regard, see Vidhu Verma, "Reinterpreting Buddhism: Ambedkar on the Politics of Social Action," *Economic and Political Weekly* 45, no. 49 (2010): 56–65.

3

LOVE THAT B(L)INDS

Relationships need constant attention and care. They do not let one rest and be at peace. If rest and peace are necessary, one has to take care of the rest of the things in life, which is of mine and of others to whom I am related and with whom my world is built. Therefore, my life is a shared one with others, so is my world. French thinker Marc Crépon in his latest work, *Murderous Consent* (2019), discusses this condition of every being in terms of "being-in-the World." Here, Marc uses the term "World," which is with capital "W," to refer to the world in the wider sense—universe or, in Derridian term, cosmopolitanism. Accordingly, my world, inseparable from the world, has a direct impact on the latter. That is why it is difficult to think of the possibility of absolute freedom of the self. The unavoidable relational character of life limits *my* freedom. In that sense, the life of being is always, as Crépon says following Levinas, a "living-with"—living with other(s), which also includes death.

Such relational existence of the being not only suggests the difference between self and the other, which appeals and enables relations but also challenges the sovereign power of the self that enables him/her to decide for the other. Being should not forget this condition of existence, which I would call, *life-in-dependence*, in its aspiration to happiness, freedom, rest, and peace. Then, *my* existence is not only about *my* happiness, *my* freedom, *my* peace, and so on but also about my infinite effort to abstain from violence against another, irrespective of my desire for self-fulfilment. Determination to abstain from violence is motivated by the concern for life—every life without considering any hierarchical or categorical difference.

However, amidst the desire for self-fulfilment—happiness, freedom, comfort, security, and success—we tend to forget, neglect, or, at times, even decide to let go of our concern for the other. Such carelessness, negligence, or decision not only paralyzes the discourse of the other but also threatens the one fundamental to self-survival, which is the discourse of responsibility.

DOI: 10.4324/9781003045212-4

Responsibility

Responsibility is always *mine* and always to the *other*. Answering Julian Wolfreys' question on responsibility during an interview conducted at the "Applied Derrida" International Symposium, Derrida presents, briefly though, his take on the concept of responsibility as follows:

> the responsibility we take, or which we want to take, is always the responsibility for the other. This is the most difficult thing to do. When I take responsibility in my name for me, and since I am not identical with myself, I've just applied to myself, then taking a responsibility for myself means that I act under the law of someone else. And I take the responsibility for myself for an other; whether in myself or outside, it makes no difference. The absolute other in myself or the absolute other outside amounts to the same thing.
> (Brannigan et al. 1996, 222)

Responsibility is the concern and the care for the other—to protect the life of the other. Such responsibility is, nevertheless, a challenge, since one does not know, because one *cannot* know, *how* to care for the other, and *how* to be responsible to the other. This ignorance due to the impossible self-appropriation of the other, however, does not absolve us from the responsibility, of which the ultimate goal is *to save the life*. Come what may, we cannot *be oblivious to* that. Hence, the collapse of such discourse vital to life could only lead to a spiral of violence weakening all other discourses related to life—hope, care, rest, and peace. This is what Shyam reminds us through his work, *The Hungry Ghosts*, which presents the inattentiveness to the responsibility to life resulting in the blood-bath in the post-independent Sri Lanka. Hence, the present chapter aims to highlight the significance of Shyam's thoughts in writing to address the question of responsibility in the context of violence and their relevance in rethinking and reinterpreting our understanding of love, care, freedom, and peace in order to create a future, if not entirely free, at least less burdened with hate, vengeance, and cruelty against life.

However, one of the things that cannot go unnoticed in this singular intervention and invention of Shyam is its intermingling with the Buddhist idea of non-violence, which is certainly *beyond* how it is defined appropriated, and practiced by any Buddhism or any Buddhist community today—*Teravada*, *Mahayana*, *Vajrayana*, *Navyana*, etc. (Dube 1980, 37–89). In fact, it is necessary to be *beyond* or *otherwise* than the perceptions held by all the Buddhist communities today regarding the Buddhist idea of non-violence. Such otherwise*ness* or beyond*ness* is urgent in order to lessen, resist, and condemn ongoing violence committed by the Buddhist communities against the other. The present scenario in the Buddhist communities of South Asia is a case in point that illustrates violence unfolding in Buddhism as well as the violent unfolding of Buddhism. Like any other worldly religion poised by the desire for their respective identities, Buddhism, too, subscribes to some form of violence for its survival. Therefore, demolishing one of the fundamental pillars on which Buddhism is founded—responsibility, today's Buddhism has become more exclusive, resistive, and inhospitable to the other.

The Buddhist idea of responsibility is decisive to Buddhist ethics and emancipation (*nirvana*).[1] Similarly, it is also relevant to the larger discourse of ethics and emancipation beyond Buddhism since it does not address any Buddhist per se. In fact, no religion is concerned with a particular addressee. The addressee could be anyone. They only *address*, and it is thus an open one. That is why/how anyone could worship any god or follow (secretly though) any religion whether that god or religion is named and identified as Christian, Islam, Jew, Hindu, Buddhist, Jain, etc. However, since Buddhism is particularly concerned with the *renouncement* of desire, which is always a desire *to acquire*, *to have*, *to own*, *to possess*—the desire for belongingness and ownership, it preempts even the desire of *belonging* to Buddh*ism*. In other words, one should not desire to be a Buddhist by *claiming* to be so because that desire is yet *another* desire. Therefore, *if* there is a *real* Buddhist, he or she *does not* belong to Buddhism *as such*.[2] There cannot be a Buddhist *as such* in terms of belonging. Along the line of this thought, one could even say there is no Buddhism *as such* in a totalized sense. Buddhism insists on the impossibility of totality—the oneness, the completeness, the fullness, and the presence. That is why the idea of responsibility preached by Buddha neither is a responsibility directed towards Buddhism nor is it towards a Buddhist *as such*. It is instead towards every human in the world despite all differences. Thus, it has a universal appeal, and Shyam's *The Hungry Ghosts* is in sync with this universal appeal in its insistence on responsibility as ethical exigency in love, care, protection, and hospitality.

"You Loved … Perhaps that Made You a Little Blind"

Love is a force that could make or mar a person or a community ranging from the smallest unit to the widest level—the universe. In other words, it is a life-taking force as much as it is a force of life-giving. Here, when I say *love*, I mean love of *any kind*: love for parents, siblings, life partners, family, community, nation, land, God, religion, food, technology, money, wealth, success, and flora and fauna. Now, in the attempt of understanding love as a force potential of both life and death, Shyam's *The Hungry Ghosts* is of great importance since it offers a profound perspective, not so much on love *as such*, but on *how* to love, insisting on the necessity of responsibility in love—love *responsibly*. So doing, it appears as a critique of self-love.

As mentioned in the previous chapter, Shivan has spread out an obituary in response to Michael's quest for truth. Face in the obituary is that of Mili, with whom Shivan had fallen in love. Though he was attracted to Mili's charming look and gestures from the school days, he could get close to him only when he made his first visit to Sri Lanka from Canada. Their first meeting was in Sriyani Karunaratne's home. Those early weeks were "magical," and they were safe, for no one knew about their relationship. The visit to Sriyani's beach house was the most "splendid time that he had with Mili (Selvadurai 2013, 171). Being a gay couple, they could meet only in secret. A relationship of that kind is not permissible in Sri Lanka.

According to the Sri Lankan law, all the lovers and their inclinations for love should ideally be heterosexual—the new *normal* and the new *natural* (Butler 1990). It has brought love under the law, commanding love to be in accordance with the law. Accordingly, love should follow the law. But, is such a thing possible? How would one manage to do that? Practically, it should be otherwise. In the sense of Levinasian terms, the law should be deduced from love. Love, like justice, being unconditional, is always outside the law (Derrida 2002a, 230–297) and cannot be conditioned by law. However, if the law attempts to impose itself on love by putting conditions on it, the law fails massively. This failure, on the one hand, is due to the force of love capable of escaping law and vigilance, escaping any judicial, political, or ideological grid. No matter how tight and strong it is, love escapes; it travels across and beyond all borders. On the other hand, the failure is due to its (own) inability to serve the very purpose that it is founded, which is justice beyond all categorical existences—*every* being.

If the law is for *justice*, *if* it operates *in the name* of justice, it is imperative that the law operates *to protect* life *by* valuing, respecting, and caring for it. It is to meet this end that the law should undergo transformations, which also means that it should expand by interrupting and un-doing its *self-invented* and *self-enforced* borders and limits. Derrida terms this ability of the law as "deconstructibility of law" (Ibid, 243)—a positive aspect that enables the law *to become* law by inventing it.

Nonetheless, when it comes to the law, in general, what we are familiar with is the respect often one-sided—from the side of the subjects towards law. Subjects are expected to respect the law by showing obedience to it since it is meant for them (Derrida 1992, 183–220) for their (own) well-being. Therefore, our actions should be in accordance with the law. It is only then one is able to access the law seeking its help (Ibid). Now, the problem here is, whether our actions and movements are *always* in accordance with law; also, whether we are always conscious of law. On the other hand, even if one does everything according to law, and, thereby, becoming a lawful subject, would that lawfulness be worthy or of use in case it amounts to be a direct or indirect contribution to the annihilation of another life? Would such lawfulness be on par with ethics? This question leads to the larger question of distinguishing law from ethics: Is law ethical always? This is one of the questions that Shyam raises throughout his oeuvre, from *Funny Boy* to *The Hungry Ghosts*, which interrogates the ethicalness of Sri Lankan laws in the way in which it intervenes to address the question of homosexuality in Sri Lanka.

In *The Hungry Ghosts*, the appeal is more audible than in any of his other works, as it is an incident of homosexuality that leads to the death of the beloved—death due to the denial of access to the law for legal assistance. The absence of legal protection for homosexuals, particularly for *gays*, especially in a time of war, terrorism, and insurgency, could make their lives even more miserable than anyone else from the same period. They are simply the outlaw and already guilty in the eyes of Sri Lankan laws for being outside the order of naturalized heterosexuality. This condition causes Mili's conscious movements with Shivan. Unlike other heterosexual couples, they were not free *to meet* as desired. The unsafe condition in the country called for by the activities of terrorists and political parties competing with each other for the hold of power had introduced various mechanisms of surveillance deployed by various groups. However, no one was able to know exactly *who* searched *whom* for *what*. It was a time where everybody doubted and rejected every other despite their identities and affiliations. Mili had realized how the cord of violence got "tighter and tighter" every day and how their relationship got affected by the same. Having fallen outside the law despite being a Sinhalese from Cinnamon Gardens, he could do nothing about it other than making attempts to express and share his disturbed mind with Shivan. Whenever he sat with Shivan at the verandah of his grandmother's house, he spoke "moodily" about the rising violence in the South committed by the Janatha Vimukthi Peramuna (JVP) and the government—about the bodies being found by the main roads (Selvadurai 2013, 173). He dwelt on the murder of a human rights lawyer "falsely arrested" by the police for the death of the actor-turned-politician Vijay Kumaratunga. According to the government press release, the lawyer, a high-ranking JVP member, was responsible for the assassination. The post-mortem of the lawyer, who died in a Colombo hospital, revealed his body to bear "more than a hundred wounds and that his death had been caused by bludgeoning with a blunt instrument" (Ibid). However, despite the love for Mili, Shivan was unwilling *to listen* to Mili's expression of discontentment, frustration, and unhappiness. Instead of giving support to Mili, he felt that Mili tried "to thwart and irritate" him by talking about the things that he disliked. Shivan disliked such talks as they "spoilt" their time together.

The "time together" being *already* less, Shivan had wanted at least *that* limited time should be *theirs*. It should involve none other than the two of them and their love for each other. This desire was furthered by some "unspoken sexual frustration" between them, and he searched for words and gestures from Mili, which not only could express love but also confirm the same. In the same spiral of desire and frustration, he wanted to know about Mili's past encounters with men, though he was afraid to inquire "directly." Hence, he approached the same question indirectly by asking "how" he had "figured out" that Shivan was gay. Yet, he could not succeed as Mili only laughed in reply. He never talked about his previous relationships. In reply, either he changed the subject or looked at his watch, declaring the need to go to his mom (Ibid). Their conversations often ended this manner, and Shivan "often curse[d]" himself for "having driven him away" by digging at his past. Mili's love was neither convincing nor assuring *enough*. It is due to two reasons: one is the *inadequacy* of assertive words and gestures that could affirm his love for Shivan; the other is the *incompetence* of the words that he managed to utter in order *to express* his love for Shivan. The lacuna in language and communication accelerated the desperateness in Shivan, causing him to act erratically. The novel offers a couple of such incidents. The following conversation of Shivan announcing his decision to stay back in Sri Lanka is one such example that brings out Shivan's dissatisfaction with Mili's response.

> "I waited until after dinner when we were seated on the verandah to announce my news. Mili was silent after I told him […]"
> "Mili?" I could not see his face in the shadows.
> He straightened up in his chair. "That's great, Shivan."
> "You don't sound happy about it."
> "No, no, I'm really happy."
> "You're not."
>
> (Ibid, 176–177)

Shyam writes about the inadequacy of the response in language, which is also, on the other hand, the inadequacy of language in response. The response, language, has not only *not* managed to communicate the intended but also, *at the same time*, has communicated the mismanagement of communication. However, as far as communication is considered, it is always *to be managed*. It also means that there is never *perfect* communication. It is due to some unavoidable gap between the beings *in* conversation. This quality is mainly of language which enjoys enormous freedom and resists belonging of any kind. It does not belong to anyone. No one could own it by speaking in it. As Derrida writes in *Monolingualism of the Other*, "it will never be mine, this language, the only one I am destined to speak, as long as speech is possible for me in life and in death; you see, never will this language be mine. And, truth to tell, it never was" (1998, 2).

One could speak only by trying to appropriate that which does not belong to him/her. It is thus an effort to appropriate the other and speak in other's language. One should speak oneself yet in other's language. Derrida goes on to argue the impossibility of such speech since one does not know how to speak and express one's self in a language that does not belong to his/her self. But, that is what we all do in communication. Here, he comes up with two propositions: "1. We only speak only one language—or rather one idiom only. 2. We never speak only one language—or rather there is no pure idiom" (Ibid, 8).

In the attempt of communication, we speak in appropriation. There can be only an appropriation in language. Yet, attempting to appropriate, we, like the mythic figure Echo, do it our (own) way, which is singular and unique. It is impossible to appropriate the other absolutely, for the otherness of the other is irreducible to *my* knowledge—*beyond*. Therefore, one could only try *to listen*, *to read*, and *to understand* the other without having the assurance of any of these *self*-readings, interpretations, and understandings being absolutely correct. In other words, one could only guess—*perhaps*. They are efforts of appropriation enabled as well as disenabled, determined as well as demanded by the very impossibility of appropriation. That is why every communication, reading, and understanding always runs the risk of being imperfect, inaccurate, inadequate, inappropriate, and so on. Subsequently, it also disallows drawing one *Final* conclusion on anyone or anything—the last word. Language thus does not close down the options or pathways. It is always open.

Now, the conversation between Shivan and Mili takes us to this complex question of appropriation. Irrespective of Mili's assertion, "no, no, I am really happy," Shivan reads Mili's unhappiness in response: "no, you are not." His perception affirms its subjective dimension. Now, one may argue, every perspective is unavoidably subjective, and each one is valid and important.

Nonetheless, my question here is whether we are ready to value, accept, entertain, and respect such subjective positions in a context like *love*?

This question, no matter how trivial or ordinary it might sound, needs to be raised here because, in common parlance, love is thought to be capable of eliminating the difference between the lovers and uniting them together as one—oneness resulted in the elimination of singularities. The unity assumed to be there between lovers is determined by this assumption. However, this assumption that raises the expectation for unity or oneness is misleading, as well as destructive. If one believes in the possibility of such oneness, completeness, or unity in love, then, at the same time, he or she has to disbelieve love because love is enabled only by difference (this idea has already been discussed in the previous chapters). Love does not erase the difference between one and the other. It *should not*. It instead holds and bears the difference together. The proximity, closeness, or intimacy in love is appealing and is anticipated only because of this difference underneath. The difference, no matter in what scale or degree, disenables fusion, unity, totality, or completeness. Therefore, two lovers, *in spite of* love, as well as *because of* love, would not have the same perception, let alone on any other thing, even on the force that has brought them and held them together—love. Here, it is necessary to mention that any love, individual or collective, is determined by this irreducible difference between self and the other.

Nevertheless, these subjective positions are often in favour of the self: self-happiness, self-protection, self-care, self-respect, and self-image—love for the self. That is why, irrespective of how convincing the display of *self-assertive* unbiasedness, non-alignment, impartiality, or neutrality in the respective concerns, it is difficult to assess the neutrality of any position declared to be held by any movement, which is motivated socially, politically, culturally, geographically, linguistically, religiously, or globally, *for* justice, equality, love, peace, and humanity.

Nevertheless, this claim does not underestimate the good intention of any such movement. Rather, it is only to suggest, in most of such situations, that the underlying intention operates in favour of the self, and that could be understood only if one unties gestures and performativities laden with, as once Gandhi termed elsewhere, the "accent" *of* democracy, *of* politically correctness, *of* euphemism, or *of* altruism.

The idea of every understanding as a subjective construction and, therefore, being difficult to ignore or deny, on the other hand, appeals to the idea of freedom in the absolute sense—freedom *to think*, *to construct*, *to express*, *to knowledge*, and *to live*. Yet, as far as freedom is concerned, it cannot be absolute. There are limits to freedom—freedom *with* limits. No one is absolutely free because everyone is undeniably a subject of some community and bound by certain limits based on the community guidelines which become the law of that community. These laws, while operating in favour of its members, are meant for the community itself to strengthen its power and enhance its potency. They, as a force, are repressive and restrictive, affecting the freedom of its (own) members. In that sense, any law of any community condones some violence on its members as a measure of ensuring the freedom of its members. Therefore, it is predefined freedom, of which boundaries are strict, resisting potential interruptions and interventions from the outside. However, as definitions of law and freedom are constructions through language, deconstruction of the same is already underway. Protests, strikes, human rights movements, riots, terrorism, and war are some of those forces, which challenge and transform existing laws and contours of freedom.

Apart from law, there is another aspect that limits freedom, which is responsibility—responsibility as morality, which is beyond and outside the concerns of any given or defined community. Here, the responsibility is the one concerned with life. It demands every individual and every community be concerned with life. Such responsibility, as Levinas, Derrida, and Marc emphasize throughout their philosophical interventions discussing violence, is determined by two conditions of life: mortality and vulnerability. It is the unavoidable exposure to death that calls for caring life. It is necessary to shoulder this call that calls for responsibility beyond, as Marc Crépon says, "the logic of necessity" (2019, 21) used in the justification of violence enacted upon another for the benefit of the self. In that sense, the desire for freedom, always self-oriented, is encountered by the compulsion for responsibility to life. In this encounter, it is the life that should triumph over the desire for freedom and happiness. No subjective construction or position can be exempted from this responsibility.

Considering responsibility as an ethical exigency, there is a tendency to relate it with the situations and affairs, which are explicitly risky, aggressive, or violent. Clashes *within* and *among* communities, protest demonstrations, illegal activities and crimes, wars fought at all levels, be they civil, international, or global, are some of the examples that show active, direct, and conscious human participation in obvious violence. These contexts often evoke the urgency of responsibility though it could be partial, hierarchical, and categorical. Nevertheless, there are some other contexts like love, friendship, care, tolerance, and generosity, which are perceived, on the surface, as non-violent or harmless, where the sense of responsibility is, if not forgotten or entirely ignored, at least, taken for granted. It is probably because the aspect of responsibility is *already* entailed in them in the sense that *to love*, *to care*, *to tolerate*, or *to be generous* is, anyway, to take the responsibility on board, at the very outset. Certainly, it is so by concept, though it could be alarming at the level of performativity. That is why Shyam's *The Hungry Ghosts* is relevant here since it evokes the memories of love, friendship, care, and generosity, which caused the death of the beloved due to inattentiveness to the responsibility of love. Though the novel offers many different stories of love, the present chapter takes only the one that of Shivan and Mili to insist on the exigency of responsibility in love, care, and friendship.

Shivan's love is full of care, tolerance, generosity, and friendship. Those are, including the ones even that of anger, jealousy, dislike, dissatisfaction, stress, and pain, underlying feelings of his gestures to Mili. Shyam lays out this complex feeling of love through Shivan's relationship with Mili in which he becomes a lover, irresponsible and unforgivable.

Shivan is caught up in between many different worlds at the same time. On one side, there is a grandmother who interferes in his life unnecessarily. On the other side, there is another world opening due to his relationship with Mili, which is a punishable offence with a jail term of ten years. At the same time, all these contexts are further subjected to other kinds of violence growing in the country. Being confronted by conflicting emotions churning within, Shivan becomes "impatient" for Mili's caress (Selvadurai 2013, 219). Such desperateness in love—not only to love but also to be loved in return—drives him to compel Mili with a suggestion of going to a house in Mount Lavinia, to which Mili reluctantly agrees (Ibid, 220).

The desire for pleasure and happiness of love blinds Shivan from seeing other realities, equally important and decisive to his stay in Sri Lanka.

One such unavoidable reality was his relationship with the grandmother, who too loved him blindly. Her love for him was such that she needed to know everything about him: *where* he went, *who* his friends are, and *what* all he did with them. Though she liked Mili in the early days of his friendship with Shivan considering the wealthy status of his father from Colombo's Cinnamon Garden, that feeling gradually drifted from her after realizing Mili's role in *Kantha* as a human rights activist. Since then, she wanted Shivan to be away from him. But Shivan failing to obey the same invited unimaginable troubles. She had begun to spy on them with the help of Chandralal. However, what is revealed to her in the process is beyond *her* imagination—their love affair and the recent visit to the house in Mount Lavinia. It fuels up her anger against "Jayasinghe boy" with "vile European blood." In her inability to accept her grandson's reality of being gay, she holds Mili responsible for the same. Shivan's confession, "It's not Mili or his blood. I live like this in Canada" (Ibid, 223), could not change her assumption.

As discussed earlier, the thirst for truth is always dangerous since one is unaware of the violence to which he or she is exposed at the moment of revelation. Moreover, one revelation could lead to many other revelations despite the will or consent of the self to hear, to see, or to know those. There is no choice but to be exposed defenselessly. Shyam's works always inform this human vulnerability to the violence of pain and despair due to their (own) desire for truth. However, in *The Hungry Ghosts*, the exposure to implicit violence is depressive, gloomy, and violent. Being barred from a vent by a compulsion *to tolerate* for a future free from hate, it screams the years of pain gathered and held in silence. Yet, in the scream, it is not only the pain that is audible but also anger and hate due to the obligation, which demands the subjection and obedience to the violence of power—tolerance, *if to meet* the desired future. Therefore, *The Hungry Ghosts* is also about tolerance and its limits, where Shyam, through Shivan's declaration of "hate" towards his grandmother, subtly engages with a critique of tolerance, highlighting its paternalistic character, which draws boundaries of tolerance.

> "You call the way you had treated me good?" My head was flooding now with a white heat at the thought of her asking that thug to spy on me, to violate Mili and my privacy. "Do you know how much I hated those afternoons in your room as a child? Do you know how much I hated going around with you on all your errands, looking at those thuppai properties? Do you think I did any of it out of love? You must be mad. I don't love you. I have never loved you."
>
> [...] She nobbled away in the direction of her bedroom, but I went after her, still speaking in that sensible, wounding tone. "If I

> had not bent to you, we would have been thrown out onto street, or so I thought as a child. And you knew I was thinking like that and took advantage of my innocence. You used my fear to get me where you wanted me to be."
>
> (Ibid)

Shyam's thoughts unfolding through Shivan's words express the problematic of tolerance without making a hierarchical evaluation that judges *who* tolerates best or *whose* tolerance is best. They resonate with Derridian take on the concept of tolerance (Borradori 2003, 85–136), in which he explains his "reservations" about the word and discourses of "tolerance." Pointing "this good old word" to have its religious roots in Christianity, Derrida firstly suggests tolerance to be a "Christian charity." Then, he explains how it is connected to the idea of sovereignty as follows:

> Tolerance is always on the side of the "reason of the strongest", where "might is right"; it is a supplementary mark of sovereignty, the good face of sovereignty, which says to the from its elevated position, I am letting you be, you are not insufferable, I am leaving you a place in my home, but do not forget that this is my home.
>
> (Ibid, 127)

It is such tolerance, which is a "scrutinized hospitality," that had been granted to Shivan since his childhood. Yet, he too tolerated the grandmother since he had other plans and desires to be fulfilled while staying under her roof. Nonetheless, the "surveillance" unavoidable to such hospitality that violates his privacy with Mili provokes Shivan to the extent that he reaches the limits of his tolerance and begins to shout at the grandmother.

Now, how to decide or judge whose tolerance is best?

This question keeps appearing throughout the novel, projecting it as a strategy of survival that suspends certain violence. It is a temporary measure, which could be taken to take care of certain situations, and definitely, it is better than intolerance. Yet, it is not a long-run solution since it cannot run long. That is what we see in this example of two people tolerating each other and benefitting each other from being tolerant to each other until the boundaries of tolerance are crossed by any of the two. When the boundaries are crossed, violence unfolds in unimaginable and ugliest forms of anger and vengeance. Such outbursts, in turn, point to a deficiency in tolerance, making us doubtful about its credibility as a concept held in esteem today in the attempts of preventing violence and building peace.

The grandmother is shaken by the revelation that sprung with the violent eruption of Shivan's tolerance. Several cracks appeared in the relationship that she had nurtured for many years, making her unstable and weak. As the writing unfolds, we realize that they were anyway to appear when the tolerance reaches its limits. When the capacity for tolerance is exhausted, there is no space for *further* tolerance. Any attempt taken to push it *beyond* could only cause eruptions. In that sense, tolerance is like a volcano in which lava is intensified. In case of an eruption, its catastrophic flow is unstoppable. The only thing one could do in such eruptive situations is to manage, not the disaster but the self. If there is any lesson or programme called disaster management, no matter how advanced it is in using technological and scientific knowledge, it could only educate us and give us strategies to manage ourselves in the situation. In a way, this is what even religion does, yet differently (this idea would be discussed in the next chapter). However, if one fails to attempt *to manage* the situation before searching for a possibility for solutions, the damage caused by the same would become unmanageable, paralyzing the possibility for solutions. Shyam informs the urgency of managing not only the disaster brought by situations and the situations caused by the disaster but also that which has the potency of causing disasters. The latter is more in demand in *The Hungry Ghosts* as a remedial step that could be taken to mitigate violence and its consequent sufferings. Here, what he demands to manage is not the outside forces anterior to being but those within its (own) self. They are the forces of love, anger, and hate of which the source is desire. The above quoted incident of Shivan confessing his hate and anger towards the grandmother is a turning point in the novel. It is so not only because of its adverse effect on other following incidents but also it being a moment, of which love becomes a destructive force. Love, like hate, could be(come) destructive if not it is enacted or given with care and respect.

Though Shivan felt "easy" after releasing his anger, it was difficult, almost impossible, for his grandmother to accept this reality, different from the one she had known. The present reality is two sided. One is her grandson is *gay*. The other is his confession of hate and anger towards her. The unwillingness to accept this truth results in driving her anger against Mili, for he has not only influenced Shivan's sexuality but also invaded her relationship with him by occupying Shivan's heart in a manner that Shivan does not love her anymore. Consequently, Shivan has become the new power capable of making her suffer without his love, care, and obedience. Suddenly, her most enduring guest to whom she extended a shelter and from whom she had not expected such harshness has appeared in front of her differently. He is no longer the same. And this difference is unbearable to her.

Nonetheless, the problem here is how she is going to respond to this difference. Would she punish him by throwing him out of her house? How would she guard herself against further wounds and damages if she continues extending hospitality further?

The above incident informs us about the suffering of the self-desiring being. Here, the cause of suffering is nothing but desire. It aggravates depending on how one tries to address it. On the surface, fulfilment of desire appears to be the way to happiness, success, and freedom. This appearance is convincing. The more it appears to be convincing, the more we are drawn in to believe in it. It is the belief. The belief is able to drive us as long as we follow it, nurture it, and hold onto it. It is like how Shakespeare's Macbeth did, following the appearances. It is only at the moment of death, Macbeth realizes how he was deceived by the appearances which were convincing and compelling. However, unlike in *Macbeth*, where the king Macbeth is deceived by witches till his death, in *The Hungry Ghosts*, Shivan's grandmother is *not* deceived till her death. Shivan explicitly tells her that he does not love her. Rather, what he had for her was hate. He had hated her in a loving manner.

Nevertheless, the confession of hate could not stop her love for him because it could not stop her from loving herself. She loved *her* happiness rather than his. To lose him is to lose her happiness, and she is unable to bear that. Hence, she bears him. Diving into the complexity of love, Shyam brings out how love often tends to become self-love. In the following, he writes how she acts *to own* Shivan like a property of hers. She plans to punish Mili by giving him a "good scare, to stop corrupting" Shivan (Selvdurai 2013, 233). Accordingly, obeying her instructions, Chandralal's thugs follow Shivan and Mili till Sriyani's beach house—the place, which they selected for their stay during the four-day trip to South. On the third day, the thugs enter the house and kidnap Mili.

> "Shivan, what has your grandmother done?" he whispered, his voice cracking with terror.
>
> There was a wound on his head and the blood was beginning to pulse up, matting his hair.
>
> He was crying out in protest, his heels squelching along the floor. His cries grew fainter as they pulled him out of the house. Once they were on the verandah, they found some way to silence him. All I heard was the thud of the men's feet in the sand and the hoop-hoop-hoop of a dove. The gate clanged shut, a vehicle started up and I finally went limp.
>
> The men let me go. I turned over, my breath harsh, and gaped pleadingly at the leader. He studied me for a long moment. "We're just poor people following the instructions of the rich, you understand?"
>
> "Where are you taking him? What are you going to do with him?"
>
> "So be very careful what you do next." Seeing my incomprehension, he added, "This is not abroad, there is no point going to the police. That will only jeopardize your friend further."
>
> (Ibid, 231)

Karma

In writing desire, Shyam writes about the danger of desire, which not only makes life miserable but also elongates *samsara* (circles of birth). Here, Shyam's writing echoes the Buddhist philosophy of desire and suffering. Both Shivan and the grandmother are deprived of their desired happiness because of their desire to please the self by desiring more happiness. According to Buddhist philosophy, it is their (own) *karma* that has caused their sufferings. Shyam brings in the Buddhist idea of *karma* in a major way in his depiction of desire and violence, in which he shows how the same concept is differently appropriated, used, applied, and followed by different individuals of the same community. It could be read, interpreted, and understood differently.[3] Depending on how it is invented during each reading, it could be used either as an initiative to lessen violence operative on each level or as means of justifying violence against others. Shyam thus offers us the possibility of two different approaches in adopting the Buddhist concept of *karma* through the voices of Shivan and the grandmother.

They both believe in the Buddhist idea of *karma*. Yet, in adopting the same to their lives, they differ from each other drastically. As discussed earlier, grandmother's version often works in her favour. It comes in handy not only to console her mind in times of pain and stress but also to justify the misery, which she inflicts on others by her ruthless behaviour. But, who could contest her version? After all, she is a Sinhala Buddhist by birth. Being a Buddhist *by birth*, she self-validates her knowledge about *dhamma* and its authenticity and accuracy. Hence, it is unlikely to be poor or different from what Buddha must have preached 2600 years ago. The novel communicates this assumption of hers, suggesting how such assumptions constitute and manifest many different discourses on and around one religion and how most of them distort the fundamentals of that religion. In a way, *The Hungry Ghosts* hints at the certain death of Buddhism in the context of Sri Lankan Sinhala Buddhism.

Nonetheless, though Shivan's version of *karma* contrasts with the grandmother's, it is closer to the one that is said to have been preached by Buddha. Shivan is not a Buddhist by birth. He does not belong to any religion per se since his parents are from two different races and religions. His knowledge of Buddhism is limited and often filtered to him via his grandmother's narration of Buddhist *Jataka* tales. *Jataka* stories are the source of his knowledge of Buddha and his *dhamma*. They are also forming the gateway which leads him to Buddhism, especially as a child. However, those narratives narrated to him in his childhood return to him in a sensible manner after Mili's death, making him understand his (own) carelessness in handling their relationship. He asks Sriyani,

> I should have taken my grandmother's discovery of us more seriously. *I*, more than anyone, *should have* known what she was

> capable of. By my stupidity I killed him. You warned me Sriyani. Why didn't I listen?
>
> (Selvadurai 2013, 239, italics added)

He regrets not listening to Sriyani, who had forewarned him about the affair. According to her, Mili's friends at *Kantha* knew that he was gay though they did not acknowledge it. And Mili could not accept that anyone knew about him since the shame and embarrassment of it would be too much for him. He had to be "blind out of necessity." Therefore, she indirectly had suggested that Shivan *should* see. He *cannot* be blind. That is why Sriyani chose to talk to Shivan so that she could make him *see* that, which he *cannot* see, *does not* see, or *ignores* to see.

She says,

> "You must make the right choice."
>
> [...]
>
> "Yes, but really you're saying I must give him up."
>
> "I'm not saying anything of—"
>
> "Then why would you tell me all this? What if I can't give him up, Sriyani? What if I love him? But I suppose, since we are two men, such love could not have much depth."
>
> Sriyani flinched.
>
> "Did you tell Ranjini and Sri to give each other up?"
>
> "That was different."
>
> "I know exactly what the difference was."
>
> [...]
>
> I looked away at the kites wheeling and dipping above Galle Face Green.
>
> "I will not give him up. I could not bear it, I simply could not."
>
> "No," she cocked her head, "I don't suppose you could." She touched my arm, "Just be careful, Shivan, please."
>
> (Ibid, 216)

If he took Sriyani's words seriously, *perhaps* he could have avoided this misery of being guilty for Mili's death, even if there would be other miseries brought by the same—giving Mili up, the option that he "could not bear." Shivan's love for Mili was such that he wanted to *have* him. The infinitive, *to have*, means *to possess*, *to own*, *to hold*, *to bear*, *to keep*, also *to eat*, or *to consume*. Accordingly, Shivan had tried to possess and bear him by holding on to him. Shyam here brings in the aspect of bearing in the context of love.

To love is *to bear*—to bear not only what one *likes/wants* to bear or one is *capable* of bearing but also to bear what one *cannot bear*. Love demands such *generosity*. In that sense, *to love* someone is not only to expect to be loved in return but also to be tormented, hurt, wounded, or, even, to be murdered by the other—violence (Menike 2020). Love is a *yes* to bear *death*, as well as *to die* in murder. However, in the case of Shivan's love, it also communicates his readiness to bear, BUT only what he *could* bear—the limitedness. It tells us not only about what he is capable of doing for love but also what his love is capable of.

He is capable of loving who/what pleases him, loves him, and stays with him. Love should address his needs and desires. Now, Mili's love is one of that kind. It makes *him* happy. So, this love is for *his* happiness. In other words, in this love, what he loves is *his* happiness. In fact, in the context of love, it is difficult or impossible to say whether one *actually* loves the other, despite the usual convincing performatives, which are read and defined as acts/gestures of love. However, this impossibility is not bad. Nor does it make love bad. There is no love, which could be named good or bad. Love disenables binaries. Cixous writes such beauty of love by writing about "the story of love, in other words the story of the other and the other's other" between "lost bodies, troubled bodies, delimited bodies" by reading *Jerusalem Delivered* in writing (1991, 78–103). Rather, it appeals us to rethink the underlying complexity beneath any expression of love that ranges from the popular, easy, and loud declaration of *I love you*—the cliché—to the most silent (probably the most audible and noisy, on the other hand) expression of death resulted in murder or suicide motivated *by/in the name of* love. This also suggests that there is more than one way to love and to express the same. Therefore, it is irreducible to any act, gesture, or word *as such*. If we fail to understand every expression *of* love and every expression *in* love *as* an *idiom* of love, and, thereby, trying to appropriate with that of mine forcefully, that deliberation becomes fatal not only to love but also to life.

In that sense, in love, there are only *untranslatable idioms*. Yet, if one loves the other and *ONLY IF* one loves the other, one should attempt to translate the untranslatable idiom, which is the other and the other's love. It is an effort infinite. This is the kind of responsibility Shyam places before us. However, it is not a simple or easy thing to do. It is too painful, exhausting, and tedious, hence demands patience *with(out)* limits. Here, the idea of patience emphasized by Shyam is different from the one related to tolerance. It is more in tune with the Buddhist idea of patience—*khanti*, which insists on extreme generosity of the self, where the self gives what is impossible to give or what cannot be given.[4]

Shivan's version of *karma* plays a commendable role in his life by transforming him within, especially after Mili's death. It persuades him to *self-reflect* his actions, making him realize the gravity of his carelessness, which has pushed him to bear the very thing and the feeling which he was not ready to bear earlier—the life without him and the pain of having to live without him. If he had listened to Sriyani and given Mili up, he would have lived only the pain of not being able to spend his life together with Mili. That is already a unbearable pain. Yet, it would have been *somehow* bearable with the realization that he sacrificed his happiness for valuing, caring, and upholding the life of the beloved. Such realization would have made him differently happy and content with *how* he loved Mili, and it would have delivered him to another life (other than the one at present) that is worthy of living. However, this *was* a possibility which he has *already* missed. By missing *that* chance, the present life has already become unbearable with self-contempt for being guilty of the death of the loved other, whose ghost keeps appearing in his dreams.

However, Shivan was late to realize that there are many ways *to love*, though they are not given. They are to be invented. Inventing is difficult, tiring, and risky. Yet, Shyam insists on the *need to invent* with utmost attention and care. It is a process in which the being is deeply engaged with its being, opening an infinite conversation between self and the other. Such engaging conversation empowers being realizing not only its mistakes but also its capacity to change *within*. Shyam encourages this conversation in writing as a way through which other(ness) of being could be invented.

Inventing takes time as it is realized through a taxing path of self-reflection. Shyam demands such deliberation as an ethical exigency, resonating Buddhist idea that suggests, *one is never too late to realize one's karma*—mindfulness.[5] So doing, he informs being's ability to make attempts not to undo the *karma* in the past but to prevent the self from repeating the same. Considering past *karma*, being is always *already* late. Shivan's being emerging through Shyam's writing presents the delay of being in realizing its delay that has led him/her to act in a certain manner. Via Shivan's situation, Shyam tells us how late he is to realize not only the possibilities of inventing other ways to love but also the possibilities of love slipping into other regions that are named and defined with the words considered as *antonyms* of love—hate, vengeance, and death. However, the significance of Shyam's writing does not lie in how he articulates the delay of beings in terms of *failure*, but in the way in which he finds possibilities enabled by this failure—condition of being late as the imperative to not to be late, henceforth and hereafter—future. It is not necessary failure is always negative. It does not always lead to a spiral of failures. Instead, it could be the founding step towards success, peace, responsibility, love, and emancipation. Such realization is possible only if one makes a sincere attempt to reflect, recall, rethink, reread, and reinterpret his/her past actions. That is why Shivan's conversation with Sriyani becomes decisive here. It returns to him every time that follows Mili's death, urging him to question his (own) self: "Why didn't I listen?" When he posed the same question to Sriyani, she had replied without holding him guilty.

> And I don't blame you for anything. You loved our Mili and *perhaps that made you a little blind*, but so were Ranjini and Sri. You

> could not have known it would come to this. If you don't mind me saying, you misjudged this country, because you are now foreign to it. You wanted poor old Sri Lanka to love and accept the person you became in Canada. But it cannot. That does not make you responsible for Mili's death.
>
> (Selvadurai 2013, 240, (italics added)

Infinite Journeys and Conversations

However, Shivan's question is not about how others saw, read, and interpreted Mili's death. If not Sriyani, there is no other who could make him responsible for Mili's death. There is neither a complaint registered in the police station about the abduction nor any evidence for the cause of death. Except for grandmother and Chandralal, the truth about the incident is known only by Sriyani. Sriyani's knowledge in this regard is subjected to a secret. It is not to be articulated, not because of her concern for Shivan but the illegality that it articulates and communicates at the moment of reporting and narrating the incident to the police. Her complaint, in that sense, would finally be the one against those for whom she wanted to protect and care—Mili and Shivan.

Shyam here raises a question concerning law and truth in which he doubts whether truth has any impact on law, even if it is one of the aspects that law aims to arrive at in its function. He is suggestive that even if truth matters to law, how it matters there is different from how it does in life. In the former, it is an aim to be arrived at, depending on how well one argues for truth, or, even say, bargains for truth, pointing to the constructability of truth, whereas in the latter, it is inextricably intertwined with life, like how the breath is for both life and death. There, it is not a matter *to* prove with the help of some external evidence and witnesses. Instead, life itself stands as proof and witness to its truths. That is why, as Shyam writes, truth in life pesters more than those invented in the due procedure of law. *The Hungry Ghosts* communicates how law invents different truths during the trial. Those are completely different from the one on which the trial is conducted or called for. In such a context, it was even more necessary to silence the truth about Mili's death. Nonetheless, it could be silenced only by inventing another different truth about the same. Such inventions are even easier during times of war and insurgency. However, a mere invention is insufficient. It has to be spread by making it authentic in and through informing the media. Post-independent Sri Lanka, especially after the 1970s, has had many such inventions about many deaths (Ondaatje 2000). Though inventions are easier, it also demands efficiency in the act because anyone could invent anything. What matters in such a possibility is how fast it could reach the media. Shyam demonstrates this socio-political, juridical, economic, and cultural reality in Sri Lanka unfolded in the last two decades of the 20th century via Sriyani's invention that comes up with a different truth about Mili's death, in which death gets a humble recognition other than the one in silence.

Sriyani discusses with her husband to decide what to say about Mili's death. In this decision, her focus is on the sentiments of Mili's parents, who are unaware of Mili's true nature—gay. "It would kill them to be confronted with their son's true nature." Therefore, she should say something different about Mili's death.

For Mili cannot be brought back, as well as for there is no proof to back up any accusation, Sriyani invents the following:

> "We shall say that Mili was spending some time at our bungalow alone. He went for a late-night swim and currents..." She rubbed her forehead. "I'll make some calls. Let friends at newspapers know about this accidental drowning.
>
> "Priya, can you call the police station in Bentota and report Mili's disappearance? I don't have the strength for that. All you have to say is he might have drowned. They will understand, and the rest will follow smoothly." She smiled bitterly. "Yes, our state machinery is well oiled one when it comes to these obfuscations. We received it well oiled already from the British."
>
> Sriyani started to walk towards her study, then stopped and stared speculatively at me, as if she had forgotten I was there. "You must get your grandmother to tell Chandralal our decision. You also need to leave." Just in case I misunderstood, she added, "Leave for Canada."
>
> (Selvadurai 2013, 240)

The invented truth about Mili's death not only provides an acceptable and respectable death to Mili and his parents but also enables Shivan's safe exit from Sri Lanka. However, in the task of inventing truth, Shivan is confronted by two different truths. One is the *invented*; the other is the one, which *actually* happened. By the time he left for Canada, the invented one had already become the real, and Mili disappeared into the other side of life, awaiting the funeral postponed until the body was found (Ibid, 244).

Shyam notes how Sriyani's response, along with the invented truth, fails to console Shivan. He was neither concerned, how truth was fabricated. Nor was he worried, how others looked at him. The only thing that mattered to him was how *he* looked at his (own) self in front of Mili's death. He was facing his own trial, in which he found him guilty for the murder—murder of a friend, the beloved, a human, and a living being. The "law of karma" had begun to torment him in a manner that he could not escape from the responsibility of accepting his blunder. Late at night, staring out the window, he went on thinking about the paths he *should have* and *could have* taken to save Mili.

> *If only* I had listened to Sriyani; *if only* I hadn't pushed Mili to visit that house in Mount Lavinia; *if only* I had taken my grandmother's anger and disgust at Mili more seriously.. *I should not have* agreed to leave the bungalow once the thugs had taken him, *I should have* phoned Sriyani right away instead of wasting time coming back to Colombo. *I should not have* trusted Chandralal. And always, always, my thoughts returned to the terror in Mili's face just before they dragged him away, his heels resisting against the cement floor. *What* did those men say to him? They *must have told* him he was to be taught a lesson for corrupting me, insulted him, called him a ponnaya. Did he *hate* me then? Did he *curse* me for putting my happiness before his safety?"
>
> (Ibid, 272, italics added)

By writing down the restlessness simmering in the inner most being of Shivan, Shyam upholds the responsibility to the other as the most fundamental requirement to ethical and truthful living. However, he differentiates this responsibility from other *given* responsibilities. Accordingly, unlike other responsibilities, the responsibility to the other *cannot* be given in advance, though all the given ones are subjected to the same. It is to be invented *ex tempore*. That is why responsibility is a *decision*. Here, Shyam's thoughts move us to some deep philosophy communicated through Buddhist *Jataka* stories. Few *Jatakas* play a commendable role in shaping the philosophy of love and responsibility emerging from the novel.

In the tiring and tearing process of self-reflection, Shivan realizes his selfishness which is similar to that of the grandmother. The words with which he had accused her in his anger echoes in him, making him realize that he is not different from her (Ibid). "By placing my happiness first, I, too, had destroyed the thing I cherished" (Ibid).

This knowledge through self-realization is certainly of no use since it cannot alter what has *already* happened. However, Shyam suggests that no knowledge is outdated or late since its significance and relevance could arise in some other time *to come*. His writing, in which *Jatakas* are weaved into Shivan's life, exhibits the relevance of the knowledge imparted by old *Jataka* stories, addressing existential problems common for all. Hence, though this knowledge of Shivan fails to undo the death of Mili, it is perhaps capable of preventing future deaths and other violence which are unimaginable yet possible.

Then, it is important to pay attention to what happens after Shivan reveals the truth. Shyam tells us how bitter life could become in the *event* of truth. It is not because there is some bitterness *intrinsic* in truth. Rather, it is because we, as humans, are unable to face it and handle it, especially when it is *not* in our favour. Consequently, we tend to bend the truth and adjust it in the way we like to have it, face it, name it, and live with it, and we are ready to justify ourselves with our versions of the truth. There is a rush in us to indulge in such adjustments so that life passes smoothly and orderly. Here, we fear not so much for life but the possibilities of life going out of order—the order that we have imposed on it to make it stable. In other words, we rush to fix a truth for ourselves before the truth comes and does its fixing. In the latter, we are unable to do much but to accept and surrender to what it brings to us. It is this reluctance and fear of facing the truth that unfolds in the novel. Each character carries this fear from within, and it makes them either run away from it by running away from people, places, and situations or makes them bargain for some bearable version by reading, translating, and naming it differently. What one needs to be sure of regarding his/her version is that it should be convincing *enough* not only to one's (own) self but also, more importantly, to others. So long as one manages to convince the other, anything could pass *as* truth.

In *The Hungry Ghosts*, Shyam shows how this tendency operates from individuals to governments to nations to the globe while highlighting its dire consequences when it fails miserably. Therefore, come what may, he upholds the significance of facing the truth by choosing to hear the truth, speak the truth, and practice the truth. It is the best practice rather than enjoying a temporary one that is managed and convinced with a lot of art and craft for the sake of happiness, success, order, stability, certainty, and freedom. Nevertheless, the practice of truth *is not* and *should not be* directed to achieve some goal. It is so because it simply cannot assure anything in return. M.K. Gandhi is one of the important figures that we should remember in recent history in discussing the significance of truth as a practice of everyday life. He has suggested it as a measure possible to be taken by every human to avoid violence. As he explains, though such practice is incapable of deciding its future fruit, it enables and empowers one with the self-knowledge which affirms to his/her (own) self that *I* am *not* guilty of betrayal, dishonesty, or murder—violence.

Now, coming back to Shivan's revelation of truth, Shyam writes how it upsets Michael as well as their relationship. It affects everyone and everything around both of them while changing them to different beings of whom they are unaware of and thus being unable to handle the unknown otherness unfolding each moment unimaginably. Being exposed to the trauma of post-truth condition, Michael begins to regret his request for truth. He says, "I wish you hadn't told me. I wish I hadn't asked. Perhaps I didn't want to know" (Ibid, 337).

Truth, the Necessity

However, Shyam says, truth is a necessary condition to love. It is the first and the last that love requires to become *true* love. Though Shivan was aware of its necessity for the last two years, he did not know how to express it. It appears *as if* he waited until the truth comes and does its fixing, including even unsettling and destabilizing the fixities. Now, when it has come in its own time, there is no way out for them but to surrender themselves to it with a *yes* to accept and bear whatever it brings in. They both are victims. One regrets hearing it, while the other regrets not only being so late to reveal it but also having to bear how the other is affected by *that* delay. In any case, Shivan does not regret the revelation. He had *wanted* Michael to know it, though he did not know *how* he would know it. He says, "No, you had to know" (Ibid).

Since then, it is the power of truth that drives Shivan to invent a different approach to both love and life. He sees how every day that came after the day of revelation had brought a different Michael to his life, and he realizes his own hand in the making of the *very* person that Michael had become. His past has tainted Michael and changed him. Hence, he is no longer the one who opened his door, as well as his life to Shivan, two years ago. "He has become someone he does not recognize" (Ibid, 370).

In the latter part of the novel, Shyam tells us about the efforts of reconciliation taken to keep the relationship going. One of the ways in which Shivan had tried doing it was, being ready to pay for Michael's master's in Asian studies, which Michael had accepted reluctantly. Nevertheless, after a few days, the old restlessness returns to Shivan because of a dream about Mili. Driven by the desire to be truthful, he shares the dream and its effect with Mili. On the other hand, his restive and aggrieved mind could not stand little habits and the messes of Michael. In his eyes, those were Michael's failures.

Even if Michael tried being patient with Shivan, he too could not bear the moody distance between them and accused Shivan of being a liar and for soiling his apartment and his life. Thus, there were cycles of quarrels and patching ups. Each time, Shivan kept telling himself that time would cure everything and we would get past this terrible period "if we both clung on" (Ibid, 342).

Peace in Difference

While writing the hard days between Shivan and Michael, Shyam lays out the tendency common to all humans, which is the *desire* to cling, to hold, to grasp, and to possess. He does not criticize the desire. Instead, he draws our attention to focus on how it becomes the source of stress, pain, and suffering. By desiring love, happiness, freedom, and victory, one does not desire pain or suffering. One desires *only what one desires*. In desiring so, one becomes the master of his/her desire in the sense that he/she knows how to address it. That is about what we do with our desire and how we want to address it. Nonetheless, in the *process*, what we tend to forget is *what desire is capable of* doing. Shyam offers us both sides: what we do with our desire and what our desire ends up doing to us, as well as to others. So doing, he reminds us of the importance of being aware of desire. One should realize that the desire needs to be moderated (whatever that desire could be), for it flows free otherwise. Such realization is necessary so that one could try inventing ways and means to canalize it harmlessly. In addressing the question of desire amidst the desire *to write*, Shyam takes into Buddhist approach via a *Jataka* story, "The Thieving Hawk" narrated to Shivan by his grandmother, "where a narrative moment became its own tale" (Ibid, 18). He writes the story.

> In it, a hawk steals a piece of meat from a butcher and rises triumphant into the sky. Soon, however, other hawks surround him and try to pluck the meat away, tearing at the thieving hawk with their beaks and claws. He tries to escape them, refusing to give the meat up, even though he is bloodied and wounded. Finally, however, his agony is unbearable and he lets the meat fall. The other birds swoop down to grab it, tearing and clawing at each other now. The thieving hawk flaps away, injured and starving, but free from the thing that caused him such suffering.
>
> (Ibid)

Shyam weaves this tale into Shivan's life, which unfolds as yet another tale, before his flight back to Sri Lanka. He remembers the story, which was firstly a narrative that narrated how desire could lead to suffering and how one could free him/herself from it, by renouncing the thing that causes the same. But, over the years, most of the narratives that he had heard had become more than narratives in a manner that it is difficult for him to differentiate narrative from life or vice versa. He does not remember when and where the two got mixed up, blurring a boundary assumed to be there.

The story of "The Thieving Hawk" reminds him of his mother in the days after his father's death. She looked exhausted but at peace. When he and his sister spoke to her, she did not shout at them and send them away. She was, instead, mild and gentle, touching their faces and arms with her fingertips (Ibid, 19).

> When my father was alive, there was hardly a night my sister and I fell asleep without the sound of our parents' fierce whispering in

> the living room or outside on the verandah, my mother crying, my father pleading. Sometimes, my mother would not be able to contain her anger and she would yell at my father, calling him a ponnaya, a faggot, railing at his weakness and incompetence.
>
> (Ibid)

However, she is a *near* example that he could think of when he thought about the story. Yet, there was something in her preventing her from becoming the best example of renouncing the desire to own and to hold. She could not renounce like how the one in the *Jataka* story did. The memory of the dead husband and his death stopped her from doing so. It, instead, made her realize her own responsibility in her husband's death and the delay to "beg" his forgiveness (Ibid, 24).

Shivan, in writing, looks at these incidents by distancing himself from the same. The distance was necessary to see, to hear, to reflect, and to understand what was going on *in* life, as well as what was going on *as* life. There, he sees and hears what others did, what they had wanted to do, and what ended up happening. These others were of two kinds: on the one hand, there was his mother, sister, grandmother, Mili, Michael, and other characters to whom he was related. On the other hand, there were communities, nations, governments, and states, which fought with each other and got divided due to differences. He saw how each of them had their own visions to address the problems that had mattered to their existence. In this struggle, some died, some failed, some ran away, some gave up, some managed to survive, and some fell sick. They each stood with a different story about the difference(s). Each one's story was an attempt to justify why their story happened to be only in the way it is said. Shyam, responding to the other in writing, brings out Shivan's story about difference, yet in a different way than the previous ones.

In the previous ones, the difference appeared to be a thing to fight, demanding eliminating difference, for it is considered to be the barrier to unity, totality, or oneness. He sees how those attempts, made wherever in the world to eliminate differences of any kind, have caused pain, violence, and misery. In every attempt, what was in danger, nothing but the *very* thing for which the attempt is initiated—the unity. It, in turn, affirms the impossibility of absolute erasure of difference. The understanding of difference, as unavoidable for being and the existence, motivates Shivan to choose differently *this time*, which comes after the years of an imposed unity. In that sense, Shivan's story is a *different* story about *difference*, in which difference is acknowledged, respected, and cared for as a way *to hope* for love and peace. Shyam conveys this hope of Shivan by placing him before the two choices offered to him by Michael after hearing Shivan's idea of going to Sri Lanka to make peace with the grandmother. His way to peace is to be begun by finding a way to seek forgiveness from her. It is this attempt at forgiveness and peace which is confronted by Michael's ultimatum.

> "Why do you have to go back? All that is past. Put it behind you and move on."
>
> "But you can't just put things like that behind you, Michael. I must come to terms with her, with everything that happened, otherwise, I, we, will never move on."
>
> Michael sat back on the sofa, his mouth slightly agape, as if exhausted.
>
> "What if she doesn't forgive you?"
>
> "She must, she will."
>
> Yet he saw I had not allowed myself to consider the alternative. "Don't be too sure. She wouldn't even pose for a photograph"
>
> "No, no, she will forgive me."
>
> "But what if she doesn't?" He stood up, strode towards the balcony as if intending to go out, then changed his mind and came to stand behind a wing chair, elbows resting on top. "I am issuing you an ultimatum. If you go and she doesn't forgive you, don't come back to me."
>
> I laughed in disbelief.
>
> "No, I mean it. You take that risk if you go."
>
> (Ibid, 346)

Now, how to face this ultimatum? Shivan weighs both options. One is to forget the past and move on. The second is to make peace with the past by asking forgiveness from grandmother by visiting her in Sri Lanka. Shyam clearly shows that he (Shivan) is not ready for the first. It is impossible. One *cannot* forget the past, even if one moves on. He is a self-witness to this difference. The second is the only option that he could try, yet without the slightest assurance of success. However, now, Michael has made even that effort difficult with his ultimatum. It warns him about the possibility of a failure. Failing to earn forgiveness from the grandmother would disallow him to return to Michael. But, from his side, the whole purpose of making this journey is only to return to Michael and build a peaceful future together for them. Since childhood, he was ambitious about a future free from hate. Yet, the path into which he fell while walking to a future of his own was full of hate, anger, vengeance, and violence. If to earn that childhood dream, it is necessary as well as urgent for him to come out of that path by inventing another in response to a call for a peaceful future. He goes on thinking, without being able *to decide* how to secure his love for Michael, which is also the expression of love for truth, life, future, and peace. It is then, he remembers the story of the "naked peréthi" and imagines the grandmother's voice telling that story.

> Ah, Puthey, three times a day, three times, her servants would lay that table. They were peréthayas as well, because of past crimes, reborn as slaves and faceless, as if a wall of flesh had grown over their features, just little holes for breathing, nothing else. These wraiths would drift in three times a day to lay the table, which stretched the length of the room and was covered in an immaculate white cloth. And three times a day that peréthi's agony would rise to new heights as she walked around the table.
>
> (Ibid, 368)

As the story reads, seeing the food on the table, *peréthi's* hunger grows. With this unbearable desire for food, she reaches one of the dishes, hoping that the curse would be lifted just once so that she could taste the food. But, the moment she puts food in her mouth, it turns into the "filth of feces and urine," making her spit out them—"maggots wriggling between her teeth." Her nights, too, are awful, for she has to lie on a hard plank. On the other hand, due to bad karma, she cannot wear any cloth, for it burns her body. However, at midnight, a cold wind comes off the sea and hits her naked body making her tremble. When it is unbearable, she runs to an ante-chamber where garments are hung in rows and walks through them without touching the clothes—Banarasi silks, Pashmina shawls and shifts, cotton gowns, and heavier silks. Her strong desire for beauty and for warmth becomes uncontrollable; she takes a garment and puts it on. However, because of the karmic effect, the momentary respite she felt with "the soft brush of wool and silk" is destroyed by a sudden heat rising through the cloth. She screams while pulling out the cloth and becomes naked again. But then, finally, one day, a ship carrying the disciple of Lord Buddha comes to her island (Ibid, 368–369).

Then, it was a story that she had narrated and left there so that he could finish the tale in his head (Ibid, 369). And he knew how it ended. But, now it returns to him at a point where he should find a way to end his suffering, which also has led to the suffering of the beloved. He goes deeper in self-reflection, in which he sees love, care, and happiness in a different way. He realizes that they all are determined by a sense of giving—generosity. Here, the idea of generosity is different from the one in the binary of giving/receiving. It emphasizes the necessity of a willingness or openness to receive unconditionally—the kind of necessity reflected in *Vessantara Jataka* in Buddhist literature, also the one emphasized in Derridian reading of Biblical event where Abraham sacrificed his son (Derrida 1995a), as well as the one reflected in writing and praying. In such generosity that is open to receive unconditionally, one cannot act in favour of self-desire. It, instead, demands the renouncement of desire, for which one should renounce the very thing that he/she desires most. And, it is the most difficult and almost impossible thing to do. There, Shivan had already failed once and lost his beloved. Now, after a few years, the same condition appears as if in a cycle. This cyclic appearance needs to be addressed this time so that it does not appear again. But, if to address it effectively, he should break from the cycle in which he is caught. Such a break would bring ruptures in, and ruptures are both violence and violent. Yet, it is necessary to prevent or avoid further violence *to come*. In that sense, it becomes a break, discontinuity, cut—violence necessary for peace. That is what he had managed to gather and understand from all the *Jatakas* that he had heard about Buddha, and *that* knowledge is more enlightening than any other knowledge, which he had gained from schools and universities, where knowledge is disciplined and compartmentalized to subjects in departments and faculties. In fact, the knowledge gathered from *Jatakas* is more enlightening than the one gained from Enlightenment. Shyam writes the thoughts going into the making of Shivan's decision:

> It is I who must give up Michael, not he who will leave me; I who must break us out of our cycle of anger, then peace, then anger again. This time, I will save the person I cherish the most by giving him up. [...] And I, like that naked perethi, will find release only by offering it to another, by putting another before myself.
>
> (Ibid, 370)

Notes

1 Five precepts of Buddhism for the laity spelled out in *Sigālovāda Sutta*, the concept of *Atthangika Magga* or noble eightfold path mentioned in *Dhammacakkappavttana Sutta* and *Vibhaṅga Sutta*, and the concept of *Pāramitā* mentioned in the *Khuddaka Nikāya* in the *Pāli* canon and in the *Prajñapāramitā sutras* and the *Lotus Sutra* in *Mahāyāna* Buddhism are some of the places where the idea of ethical responsibility is discussed in detail.

2 Mahatma Gandhi and his idea of truth and non-violence are in sync with the Buddhist idea of truth and non-violence, and he practiced it as *dhamma* of his everyday life, where he valued and cared for every being without succumbing to any categorical existence *as such* marked by caste, class, gender, age, color, race, religion, and language. However, for Gandhi never claimed himself to be a Buddhist, it has been difficult to view him *as* a Buddhist. Yet, the problem that arises here is whether Gandhi was concerned at all to claim whether he is Buddhist or non-Buddhist and thereby belonging to any religious identity as such. For a better understanding of the Gandhian way of thinking and living, see Mahatma Gandhi, *Hind Swaraj or Indian Home Rule* (Ahmedabad: Navajivan, 2000); Ronald Duncan, *Selected Writings of Mahatma Gandhi* (London: Faber

and Faber Limited), https://www.yumpu.com/en/document/read/10245404/selected-writings-of-mahatma-gandhi; Sa, *The Essential Writings of Mahatma Gandhi* (Delhi: Oxford University Press, 1991).

3 Dube offers a detailed account of how the "difference of interpretation over *Dhamma*, *Vinaya*, and *Prātimokṣa*" provided a "valid ground for the occurrence of schism," which caused divisions in the original order of the *sangha*. See S.N. Dube, *Cross Currents in Early Buddhism* (New Delhi: Manohar Publications, 1980), 40–80. Similarly, commenting on "Buddhism and the Idea of the Self," Obeyesekere discusses how European thinkers and scholars have studied and interpreted the idea of the self in Buddhism, though those interpretations are not necessarily true or applicable to the Buddhist idea of "*atta*." See Gananath Obeyesekere, *The Buddha in Sri Lanka: Histories and Stories* (London: Routledge, 2018), 229–248.

4 *Vessantara jataka* story is one of the best examples to understand the idea of generosity explained by Buddha, in which he narrates how prince Vessantara wanted to attain perfection in *giving* (*dāna*) by giving all that was precious to him away. Accordingly, he gives away his two children and wife to a greedy Brahmin called Jujaka. The story could easily be read on https://static.sirimangalo.org/pdf/vessantara.pdf.

5 See what Buddha preached while commenting on jealous queen, Magandiya's violence against queen, *Samavati*. *Dhammapada* verses, 21, 22, and 23, *Samavati Vatthu* in *Appamada Vagga*. Accessed September 08, 2021. https://tipitaka.fandom.com/wiki/Dhammapada_Verses_21,_22_and_23_-_Samavati_Vatthu.

4

FUTURE (FREE) FROM HATE

Freedom matters to everyone, including the dead regardless of all constructed categories of caste, class, religion, race, colour, gender, language, ethnicity, and so on. However, when it comes to freedom, it, too, is categorized like how people are categorized and divided in society. Accordingly, we have categorical freedom*s* such as political freedom, economic freedom, linguistic freedom, and racial freedom—freedom with adjectives. Such freedom*s* are often viewed as right—right to freedom. The idea of freedom as a *right* suggests the possibilities of gaining it, losing it, and granting it. If it is losable and grantable, there should be someone or something that could grant it to another. Then, the question here is, *who/what* could grant it to *whom* for *what*? *Who/what* has the power to do that? On the other hand, if it could be granted by someone/something to another, it should be seen as an object, which is already made and, thus, could be given to anyone and taken or rejected by anyone. Such objectification of freedom proposes the definability of the same. If freedom is definable *as such*, it again takes us back to the question of *who* and *what*: *who* defines *what as* freedom, and *this* question directs us to the larger question of power and the powerful: who has the power to define *what* freedom *is*—the reason of the strongest.[1]

When freedom becomes granted by someone at the request of another, it never matches with the desired freedom of the requested. There is always some difference between the two, and that causes discontentment or dissatisfaction in the receiver. Such discontentment leads to disputes, disagreements, and resentments against both the giver and the given, sourcing struggles and revolutions for further freedom. This asymmetry, unavoidable to every context concerned with categorical freedom, is due to desire, which cannot be addressed and quenched by another since it is always a desire for the other (Derrida 2001b). Every struggle for freedom expresses some unquenchable desire, and it makes already achieved freedom *in*complete.

DOI: 10.4324/9781003045212-5

Colonization and Freedom

Now, it is such a desire for freedom that appears through Shyam's writing. It communicates the doomed condition of humans even after achieving freedom after years of struggles. This discontentment is both individual and collective. Be it in Sri Lanka—a country from the Third World, or in Canada—a country from the First World, the human struggle for freedom and happiness continues. In a way, Shyam seems to suggest that there is no country, no job, no house, no relationship, no government, and no culture that could offer freedom and happiness to humans as desired.[2] Every country, every job, every house, every relationship, every culture, every government, and every structure has had its flaws in addressing the common question of freedom and happiness. These flaws are not necessarily negative or regressive, for they, on the other hand, keep the effort going in order to make it better in the future. However, as Shyam writes, most of us from British colonies of South Asia are of the illusion that the First World could offer us a better life of liberty, happiness, wealth, health, success, and peace. It is this idea, certainly a myth like any other myth about the other parts of the world constructed by the Orientalist discourse, which motivates people to migrate from the so-called Third World to the First World. Now, one may disagree with this idea, considering the plight of those like Shivan and his family, who migrated to Canada, the USA, Australia, and parts of Europe to escape socio-economic, political, cultural, and linguistic discriminations that they underwent in their homelands.

Considering people who migrated to other countries from Sri Lanka, especially since the 1970s, they often quoted ethnic tension and war as the immediate reason for migration. It implies that *if* there were no war or racial animosity, they would not have migrated from Sri Lanka; instead, they would have stayed back. This could be a possibility, yet only with a handful of them. There must have been those who did not want to move out from their motherland if there were no such war. However, this cannot be the case with the majority of Sri Lankan immigrants. In other words, what I am trying to emphasize here is—war or ethnic tension is not the ONLY driving force behind migration, though it is undeniably one of the major. There are other reasons which could be read, in Paranjape's terms, as "enactment of desire-fulfillment" (Paranjape 2001, 6) encouraged, especially by colonial constructions about both West and East, in which the latter was often underestimated, cornered, mocked at, and discriminated due to *difference*. Accordingly, our minds are colonized in a manner that we tend to believe *what* we are made to believe as *truth* or as *right*, even if that belief is all about underplaying cultures, practices, languages, rituals, or values that we are born to and grew up with.[3] Shyam underlines this tendency of the colonized via Shivan's thoughts on fellow Sri Lankans lived in Canada:

> When the new semester began, my sister joined York's Sri Lankan Students' Union. Otara was secretary, and her fiancé, Jaya, was president. There were enough such students at York by now to form a union, so great the exodus after the 1983 riots—not just Tamils but Sinhalese and Muslims as well, *who saw no future for their children in the country*. There were also a Tamil Student's Society, its members Tiger supporters and believers in the independent state of Eelam. Otara and the union looked down on the society. Soon Renu, too, was claiming in with comments such as, "Eee, instead of fighting for Eelam, they should fight to promote deodorant among their members," or, "Eee, hasn't anyone told those Yalpanam types that coconut hair oil stinks.
>
> (Selvadurai 2013, 116, italics added)

As discussed in the second chapter, Shivan and the family, too, had those other reasons when they decided to move to Canada. However, this is not to say that the West or the White are solely responsible for such a colonized mentality of those from the colonies. To invade, colonize, control, and rule are the intentions of colonizers, and they do it somehow by using all means, even if those could be extremely violent. In such a situation, we as people from colonies must not have had any other way out but to surrender forceful subjection physically. However, in the process, subjection goes beyond the physicality and becomes mental too especially, when the period of colonization prolongs and becomes the order of the society, ultimately. It becomes *normal*, and the subjects get used to it to the extent that they tend to forget the very subjection and become the agents of the very power which dominates and subjects them to the system (Foucault 1991, 1997). In such a process, we are, consciously or unconsciously, both subjects and agents of the power that represses us. Nevertheless, as far as the mental subjection is concerned, it is more to do with our selves depending on how we look at and perceive things around us and given to us, since it is within us and cannot be man-handled like how our bodies could be. In other words, the mind could neither be imprisoned nor could it be colonized unless we make ourselves believe, follow, agree, or buy what is given to us or imposed upon us. This is not to say that the mind cannot be influenced if we remain conscious. Instead, it is to say something about our consciousness when we say or think that we *are* conscious. Our inclinations *to accept*, *to believe*, *to follow*, *to agree*, *to appreciate* or *to reject*, *to resist*, *to disagree*, *to disbelieve*, and *to question* something or someone are determined by our consciousness. Therefore, it is not about whether we could stay unaffected mentally depending on the circumstances; it is, instead, about how we react or respond following the effect. The effect is not in our hands but in reaction or response.

Our reaction or response reflects how colonized our minds are and how Eurocentric we are in our thinking (see Paranjape 2018, 101–117). Commenting on British Raj and its effect on the Indian mind, M.K. Gandhi offers a profound philosophy of *Swaraj* and non-violence in *Hind Swaraj*, insisting on human's capacity to resist colonization and subjection at the mental level rather than at the physical level. He argues how such freedom at the level of thinking could lead to other kinds of freedom, including the one concerned with the political (Gandhi 2000). Colonization could flower and prolong so long as people are colonized in terms of ideas and thoughts rather than physical control or confinement imposed on them by force. It is subtle but effective and long-lasting. One has to explore and invent a way to communicate a message to the other softly yet convincingly. It is such effective communication that is at work in the successful mechanism of Western colonization. Accordingly, though English rulers left their colonies at the end of the 20th century both physically and technically, the Empire continues in terms of ideas. Consequently, former colonies of the British Empire, some or the other way, have become extensions of English not only in governance, law, and administration but also in culture, education, and thoughts that reflect Eurocentricism with varying degrees. In this regard, the argument placed by the Indian mathematician C.K. Raju about "academic imperialism" in India is of utmost importance. In his research paper titled, *Ending Academic Imperialism: A Beginning*, he emphasizes how colonialism has "changed the system of education as a key means of containing revolt, and establishing Western rule". As he argues,

> Unlike ordinary imperialism [...] academic imperialism is self-perpetuating. Common people, too, seek Western education for the economic benefits it might entail at the individual level, through proximity to the rulers. Thus, they acquire the attitudes and values the West wants them to have. *The soft power of the West is a stronger basis for imperialism than its hard power which is otherwise vulnerable.*
>
> (http://ckraju.net/papers/Academic-imperialism-final.pdf, p. 2)

Now, this condition explained by Raju is common to all of us in the former English colonies from South Asia. To date, most of us like seeing ourselves in the light of how we have been projected by the West. In *that* light, we are *yet to be* modern, sophisticated, and advanced as people, communities, societies, and cultures.[4]

Now, these constructions matter, especially when people from South Asia decide to migrate to Western countries. They move from here to there for better prospects, which could ultimately deliver them to happiness and freedom—a "new future" (Selvadurai 2013, 88). As Shyam writes, even though that "new future" begins with a filthy site of some "open drain" nearby as the reality of everyday life, immigrants from countries like Sri Lanka and India still seem to like that kind of life rather than the one they had left behind in the lands from where they had come. Shivan sees this paradox during his walks beyond the bridge over the culvert (Ibid, 90).

When in a land like Canada with high global recognition, many immigrants like Shivan and the family are ready to bear a site, gesture, or life, which they must not have tolerated at least for a few seconds in their native lands. They give themselves to hardships with the hope that life would soon become better. There, they do not demand because they *cannot*. Instead, they accept or, should I say, even *chose* to lead a hand-to-mouth existence to save money for a future with happiness and freedom. Shivan's thoughts on life in Canada as an immigrant bring out this gloomy side that lies beneath life, which is otherwise projected as bright, free, and cool in magazines, prospectuses, reality shows, movies, etc. (Ibid, 107). In those thoughts mostly occur in isolation, Shivan seems to question the whole purpose of migration. More, he sees the difference between the expected and the existing, the more he realizes the uselessness of such a move taken by millions of families, including his. Neither the country and its people nor its culture and education could offer them their imagined freedom and happiness. This failure is not intentional from the side of the host country and its people. Rather, it is a condition of every human in the world. No one could offer freedom and happiness to another, for no one has it at his/her disposal. Instead, everyone, whether from the First World or the Third World, should find them alone. It is a lonely battle not only till death but also beyond death. In *The Hungry Ghosts*, Shyam offers this deep philosophy common to every being despite all differences that are marked racially, socially, culturally, economically, politically, religiously, linguistically, or geographically. It is this realization that makes Shivan, his mother, and sister untie the mental construction which they had liked once with much enthusiasm, and this dis-assembling delivers them to yet another Canada, which is no more a "blessed country" but a "shit of a country." In such deconstruction, once *the* best decision becomes the "big mistake" in another time. They realize the impossibility of becoming Canadians *at heart* despite being Canadians *by law*. At heart, they are South Asians, particularly Indo-Sri Lankans, whose values and approaches to life are largely shaped by the cultures and traditions that are different from those from the West—Sri Lankan–Sinhala–Tamil–Hindu–Buddhist. They are *unable* to forget them completely even if they try to appropriate other cultures and traditions. Shyam depicts this discomfort better through Hema's frustration with her two children, especially when she finds her daughter's affair with Jaya, who is already in a relationship with Otara. "We should never have come here, never. Look at what this country has done to Renu. Why else would she have acted this way? I made a big mistake bringing you children here" (Ibid, 124).

These contradictory forces make them realize how (dis)placed they are in terms of land, culture, religion, language, race, colour, gender, and so on. They are neither Sri Lankans nor Canadians, but Sri Lankan–Canadians, struggling in between or among two or more different worlds at the same time. Commenting on the condition of the South Asian Diaspora, Paranjape terms such existence as a situation of "one foot in Canada and a couple of toes in India" (2001, 161–170). The question here is how to bear this life and the living that always trembles at the edges in between?

Shyam tells us such living is *not* living but dying without death.[5] In that sense, living is about dying while bearing life for death or vice versa. Blanchot has given a great deal to unravel this confusion about life and death where he miserably fails to define one without the other (Kaushal 2016). In a similar gesture, Shyam too acknowledges the impossibility of defining what life is or what death is. He writes this impossibility of life without death and vice versa while writing about beings that occur in the infinite spaces in between. There, each being appears as being in transit, waiting to cross from one side to the other, waiting till the time comes *to cross*. If anyone could know when that time comes, one would not wait, for waiting is painful (Blanchot 1997). It is this pain in waiting without death, which compels one to commit suicide so that one is no longer obligated to wait for death but takes a hasty leap from life to death as if death is the most awaited life. Shyam throws light on this unbearable aspect of life via Hema's frustration intensified after arriving in Canada. She makes a request to Shivan that concerns her life *after* death. "I wonder what these people must have felt, dying in this country. If I die in this godforsaken country, please don't scatter my ashes here. That would be unbearable." (Selvadurai 2013, 125).

New Spirituality

Life in Canada could tell Hema only about her failures in life, convincing her that life is nothing but a series of failed attempts. When every attempt taken for a life full of happiness and freedom failed, she had decided to leave the life *for* freedom, as if it is the life that fails her in achieving freedom, as if life is the biggest enemy of freedom. Thus, she tries to free herself from life by attempting suicide. Yet, it too becomes abortive and adds to her failures. In any case, it is debatable whether one could free oneself from life or suffering by committing suicide. Is it an attempt of freeing oneself from life or an attempt of wanting to hold onto a life of one's desire?

However, when all the paths chosen for a life free from pain and suffering failed to guide her and bring her to the desired goal, Hema finally finds a "new spirituality" that guides her "to the Bodhisattva's Way of Life" (Ibid, 301). This new spirituality provides her "a way to step beyond her history, to see her life clearly, with all its problems and mistakes" (Ibid).

Shyam tells us how Hema came across this new spirituality in Canada. Accordingly, it is while working in a doughnut shop in Canada that she finds the first direction leading to freedom. Finally, Canada has been able to offer her not the freedom that she had imagined she would gain by being there but a direction, which could take her to freedom if she is ready to follow it—"a brochure for a Buddhist meditation centre" with the title, "Why We Suffer and How to End Our Pain" (Ibid, 284). The centre's philosophy is based on the teachings of a Tibetan Lama.

As far as the philosophy at the centre in Canada is considered, it is not a philosophy from Canada. Canada here is only a host that hosts a philosophy coming from outside—India. It was only because of what India could offer to the world more than 2500 years ago that Canada has been able to host it, receive it, as well as re-offer it to anyone who comes there—Canadians, Americans, Japanese, Chinese, Sri Lankans, Indians, and so on. Buddhism has been known for its openness to everyone irrespective of caste, class, race, colour, gender, language, or culture. It is that openness based on The Four Limitless Qualities—loving-kindness, compassion, joyfulness, and equanimity (Ibid, 286), which made it a philosophy of non-violence.

However, Hema was already exposed to this philosophy of non-violence via Sri Lankan Buddhism, though that exposure could not help her much, let alone to become non-violent, at least to make her realize how violent she is. This failure is not entirely hers. It is hers, as well as of others to whom she got exposed since childhood—her mother, father, relatives, and others in the society. From home to society, she could see violence in different forms despite her background being a Sinhala Buddhist. What unfolded there could not reflect any thing deeply Buddhist in attitude or practice, *dhamma/dharma*, though Buddha and his teachings have been "in the market place" in urban Ceylon since the 1960s to promote "Buddhist nationalism" (Obeyesekere 2018, 300–306). Shyam depicts his characters, especially those of Hema and Daya, in a way, it makes us re-think the background in which they are born and brought up—Sinhala Buddhist society. Both the characters hint at how Sri Lanka, which is a predominantly Buddhist society, has failed to cultivate the practice of non-violence firstly among individuals from the same community—Sinhala Buddhists.

As Buddhism is the religion of the majority Sinhalese, it is omnipresent. Buddhist temples and statues erected in large numbers throughout the island, saffron-robed monks, everyday sermons by monks broadcasted by various radio and television channels, nationwide *bodhi-poojas* and almsgivings especially on full moon *poya* days, like *Wesak*, *Poson*, and *Esala*; relic exhibitions; white-clothed laity, who observe *sill* on *poya* days; and the *dhaham pasal* (Sunday schools for children to learn Buddhism) breath out certain Buddhist*ness* active at the base of the society. And, one may believe that the Buddhist*ness* mentioned above is nothing but the one about compassion, non-violence, harmony, and peace. However, Shyam interrupts this popular discourse, which gives more importance to display *how* Buddhism is valued, venerated, protected, and promoted in Sri Lanka, rather than reflecting on whether any Buddhist teaching is followed by its people individually and collectively as an everyday practice of life, creating a society of non-violence. So doing, he proposes the urgency of inventing a different Buddhism other than the one, which is already in the dominant and popular discourse in the country, to protect every life through the practice of non-violence—*ahimsa*. Nonetheless, Shyam emphasizes this invention as a responsibility to be taken individually. It could flower only with a sincere effort taken by each individual through self-practice of *ahimsa*. Buddhist five precepts provide a strong foundation to practise *ahimsa* through self-conduct via self-restraint[6]. However, as Shyam writes, Hema or her children could not see any such self-conduct either at home or outside. This lacuna had affected all of them differently, causing them to develop self-hate from within over the years.

Nevertheless, isolated life in a foreign land brings Hema in close contact with her inner being. It enables her to see her sufferings as a result of her *karma*. The pamphlet of a Buddhist meditation centre appears in front of her eyes at a time she has been burning with rage due to Shivan leaving home secretly to live in a room at the YMCA (Selvadurai 2013, 284). It offers her a chance to take the path of "self-righteousness." Anyhow, such a path is possible only if one is ready to acknowledge one's own weaknesses not only in actions but also in thoughts and attitudes. Here, Shyam, through Hema's feelings pressed tight against each other in her first meditation session at the centre, brings to light the inner difficulties that could prevent the being, let alone following it as a practice of everyday life, but entering this path.

She was irritated by her neighbour, who was a man "short and stocky." Even if she tried to concentrate on her breath, she was unable to do so because of this typical white man, so "brash and cocky." She remembered the nonsense of the White at her work place, who always think they are better than others. Her anger at Shivan, her humiliations at the law firm, and the indignities she faced at the doughnut shop fuelled up her anger at this man. However, when she was about to blast at him, the bell rang. With the unexpressed anger, she felt exhausted (Ibid, 285).

> The sermon that day was on something called "The Four Limitless Qualities: Loving-Kindness, Compassion, Joyfulness and Equanimity." The bhikshuni went on to talk about the enemies of

> these qualities: attachment and hatred being the enemies of loving-kindness; pity, foolish compassion and cruelty the enemies of compassion; overstimulation and jealousy the enemies of joyfulness; indifference and self-righteous bigotry the enemies of equanimity. The measured tone of the bhikshuni tightened my mother's anger until she wanted to get up and yell at the woman to speak with greater animation. Once the sermon was over, the acolyte tinkled her bell to announce a tea break, after which bhikshuni would take up questions. My mother stood up, grabbed her coat from the chair back and shoved her arms into the sleeves.
>
> […]
>
> Soon she had left the centre behind. As she bustled along a quiet street, coat pulled tight about her, arms crossed, feeling humiliated as if she had made a public spectacle of herself, she silently cried, "Why did I submit to such foolishness?" But then, as she neared her house, she found herself chuckling at how over-the-top her anger was, how completely out of proportion to anything that had been done to her at the Buddhist centre. "Oh, Hema," she laughed, "you fool, you poor fool."
>
> (Ibid, 286–287)

This incident is an event that could transform Hema from within. It *turns* her from herself so that she goes outside of the self by going inward—the abyss of being. She should take a distance from her so that she could see, hear, feel, think, and look at her life from (a) different point(s) of view(s) —"multi-jective."[7] It is only then she could address herself *as if* she is addressing another by calling out the name—Hema: "*Oh Hema*" […] *you* fool, *you* poor fool" (italics added). She should see the "fool" in her, who "lacks intelligence or good judgement" Yet, this is the most difficult thing to see and to know in the context of self—to realize the fact that *I* could go wrong in *my* perception and understanding of the other. This realization could occur only when one understands his/her imperfection as being, whose life is determined by a mass of emotions, which are struggling against each other as if in a competition to rise above all and control being—mind, thinking, thoughts, body, and reactions. The sermon on The Four Limitless Qualities that Hema heard at the centre is about emotions, which become one's enemy. Those prevent the self realizing his/her ignorance. It is the ignorance that hinders being inculcating ethical precepts mentioned in Buddhism: sympathetic joy, equanimity, compassion, and loving-kindness.

Then, it is more important to realize one's own imperfection or incompleteness before jumping to judge how imperfect others are. This awareness of being *imperfect* because of ignorance empowers the being to look inward so that it sees, it *cannot see*. This failure in seeing informs a weakness inherent to sight or vision—myopia. Every vision or sight suffers from certain myopia. Therefore, every vision, no matter how perfect or clear it might appear to be, is imperfect, even if that imperfection cannot be calculated or measured. It is so especially because no one knows what it is like to be perfect in the context of being—the degree or the measure that confirms the perfection in being. The impossibility of defining the perfect being or the perfectness *proper* to the being disallows defining imperfect. However, it does not mean, being *does not* see at all, *should not* see at all, or *cannot* see at all. It instead suggests the inadequacy in every seeing, sight, vision, or knowledge. There is nothing being could do about it so that it could see adequately or know adequately in seeing. Yet, there is one thing that every being could do regarding this problem of seeing, and that is to be self-acknowledged regarding the blindness inherent to being in seeing—seeing being and being seeing. This undertaking to self-acknowledge the blindness within enables and encourages the being *to see* or *to train* its eye *to see*. Being could (s)train its eye to see even if it suffers from myopia. After all, myopia is not negative though it is a weakness because it somehow helps to see. On the other hand, it is the only way to see, especially when it is dark around. Though every seeing suffers from such inadequacy disallowing the seeing to be right—a right vision or understanding—the being could attempt making it *righteous*. Being has the ability to see or think *righteously*. Righteous seeing, righteous being, or righteous thinking is determined by the utmost concern or care for the life of being, and this concern should be born from the depth of one's heart—self-righteousness.

Self-righteousness in "ways of seeing" and "ways of being"[8] cannot be taught. One should learn it alone, even if such learning may require certain unlearning of some knowledge gained previously. It is thus a battle that being should take up against its being who has got used to certain ways of seeing and being, and, therefore, who is not ready to be open up to another or different way of seeing and being, especially because of some fear that other ways of seeing and being might not be in favour of the same—sameness in being. But, who says that the change or the shift does not favour the self? Considering the idea of self-righteousness in the Buddhist point of view, it does not imply that the being should renounce its being in the absolute sense. Rather, it is about liberating the being from desire, for it is desire, which makes him/her suffer. There are multiple desires in being. But, all those desires are finally directed to a bigger desire that desires self: self-happiness and self-freedom. However, if the being is strongly attached to its being, it is impossible to achieve happiness and freedom. In other words, so long as the self remains identical to its being, it could neither be happy nor could it be free. Nevertheless, as Shyam projects, this conundrum could be understood and solved with the help of certain guidance from someone who is said to have liberated himself from such burdensome desire that desires self by holding onto self-sameness—Buddha.

Siddhartha Gautama is an exemplary figure, who could go outside of self by taking an inward journey, which begins with self-questioning. What mattered to Siddhartha's concern was different from the one with which Western philosophy was concerned. The latter was primarily concerned with the question of "What is being?" or "What is self?" This question of "what" or "who," as Derrida discusses in *The Margins of Philosophy* (1982), is problematic at the very outset, since it presupposes the presence of being *as such* or self *as such*—the question of *essence.*[9] Contrastingly, the concern of Siddhartha begins with *doubt* and uncertainty. Accordingly, his exploration is not on the question, what *is* being or what *is* self but *whether* there is someone/something that could be isolated and identified as *self.* It thus questions the *thingness* of *self*—a question that problematizes the idea of "essence," "core," or "as suchness" of being, highlighting the impermanence of things due to "unremitting change" (Obyesekere 2018, 229–248). Accordingly, the conscious act of calling the self into question is not only the Buddhist way for the liberation of being—*nirvāna*—but also the gateway, which guided *Siddhartha* to achieve the Buddhahood.

However, the demise of Buddha marked the absence of a guide or a teacher who could guide fellow beings, including *sangha* for self-liberation from suffering. Explaining "cross currents in early Buddhism," S.N. Dube offers a detailed account by referring to *Samyutta Nikāya* on why and how Buddha "finally decided to not to appoint any successor after him and laid down that the *Dhamma* and the *Vinaya* ought to be taken as the teacher thenceforth" (1980, 43). Anyhow, Dube notes, according to the Ceylonese chroniclers, how the Buddhist community split into 18 sects or schools within a couple of centuries of the Buddha's demise due to the differences that they held in defining *dhamma* and *vinaya.* These transformations that have been happening so far have disenabled anyone or any sect being/becoming the holder of authentic Buddhism. By now, there are many versions of Buddhism coming into being through the process of re-inventing Buddhism through reading, re-reading, redefining, and rewriting canonical and non-canonical Buddhist texts. Accordingly, all Buddhists in contemporary times are guided by the *dhamma* written in texts. Buddhist texts, be they canonical or uncanonical, are capable of guiding the Buddhists, as well as the non-Buddhists. In that sense, Buddhist texts are, like any other text, open to anyone.

This openness welcomes anyone, who makes efforts singularly to enter those texts by reading and writing them. It is this openness of a text beyond all authority that welcomes and guides Hema to a "new spirituality." *A Guide to the Bodhisattva's Way of Life* has been able to move her to a path of "self-righteousness." She has been moved by the text, making her step beyond her past. Now, being distanced from her past, she is able to look back and see herself closely. This distantly close look helps her to see her problems and mistakes, which have become the source of the agony. More, she is drawn to the text and fascinated by the same, the more she withdraws from her being (past) to the one who is being transformed and invented in and through the text—reading and writing. The present one, who is also the one on the move, is more fascinating than the one from the past. It is this fascination towards the momentary being which makes her live in constant contact with self-righteous quoting from *A Guide to the Bodhisattva's Way of Life*.

Here, Shyam makes a unique intervention in his proposal to follow Buddha's way for self-liberation by suggesting some other ways to approach Buddhism other than going *only* by the cannon, which continues to debate on what is *dhamma* and what is *vinaya* according to Buddha or what is authentic Buddhism and what is inauthentic. Certainly, he does not mention anything on Buddhist canonical texts. He does not refer to any text *per se* while writing a certain Buddhist idea of love and compassion through non-violence. In fact, it is the absence of a specific reference *as such*, which makes the Buddhist undertone in *The Hungry Ghosts* audible, as well as acceptable and agreeable. It is more audible and appealing than (m)any other texts, which are meant to promote Buddhism *as such* and to direct people for the same. In that sense, *The Hungry Ghosts* is about *other* ways of approaching Buddhism, as well as *other* ways of becoming Buddhist without identifying oneself with any Buddhism *as such*.

What are the *other* ways of approaching Buddhism?

Shyam here, via Shivan, offers us two ways: one is through *Jatakas*, and the other is via other books that talk about Bodhisattva's way of living. Considering these two sources, they are stories, which narrate how Bodhisattva lived life through many cycles of birth. In each birth, he takes a different form, and that form is not necessarily human. However, each form communicates a deep philosophy, which explains how the *karma* of previous births influences the present life and how the being could liberate self of *karmic* effect through strong determination to undo them by self-practice of *paramitas*. As discussed in the previous chapter, Shivan's first exposure to Buddhism is via *Jatakas*, narrated to him by his grandmother. It is a childhood exposure. The other exposure is as an adult who went through so much suffering. And that exposure is through his mother, as well as through the lines from the books she read. Thus, the first is a memory, which keeps appearing, depending on the situations and circumstances to which he gets exposed every day as an adult. However, the second is not a memory but his mother, to whom he is exposed either in person or via telephone conversations. She is, therefore, more than a story. She is both the story and the guide to the story. Yet, she does not guide anyone but herself, and Shivan is exposed to this self-guiding being, especially when he starts to clean his mother's room. He sees a photograph of her "guru" kept on the table—an emaciated Tibetan monk with a shaven head, seated cross-legged, and one hand raised in benediction. By the sides of him, there are statues of bodhisattvas from the Tibetan pantheon (Selvadurai 2013, 301).

In the room, there is no guide in person. Neither mother nor her guru, not even the guru of the guru—Buddha. There are only images in different forms that present both presence and absence of a guru. They remind the need of a guru even in the form of an image—tradition of *guru–shisya* unavoidable to ancient Indic tradition of knowledge. This necessity does not suggest that *shisya* is always ignorant, when compared to *guru*. It is not about the hierarchy in terms of knowledge. Rather, it informs what is fundamental to knowledge, self-knowledge—difference. It proposes the impossibility of knowledge without the presence of the other. It is so, because *I* cannot learn from myself—self-sameness. There should be some other too who creates certain outside which is unfamiliar to *my* knowledge. The presence of the outside/other suggests the possibility of difference—a difference in seeing, hearing, speaking, thinking, and living—in being. Then, the knowledge confirmed by self-sameness is the same knowledge, which does not introduce anything different. It remains the same and does not allow being learning something other than what it *already* knows *as* knowledge, wisdom, or truth. There is always outside—outside *my* knowledge. And, this outside could be brought to me only by some other who is *different* from me. The otherness could be either in myself or from outside. Now, such a tradition of *guru–shisya* facilitates knowledge not only through listening, hearing, or seeing but also through interaction, interruption, conversation, argument, debate, and negotiation. Thus, the very tradition of knowledge is already one that not only necessitates the presence of the other to enlighten the self but also promotes co-creation of knowledge. The journey of Siddhartha in search of truth is an example, which shows the significance of a guru to learn and to know. Though he attained Buddhahood by himself due to his strong determination and dedication, the knowledge and the wisdom gathered from his teachers, too, helped him succeed from the attempt of knowing the truth. That is why he decides to visit his teachers soon after attaining the Buddhahood. His intention was to acknowledge and pay tribute to the great service and the help they had extended to him when he had approached them in search of the truth.

However, the guru or guide could disappear, but the teachings could become the guide in the absence of a guide *as such*. Buddhist books in Hema's room carry those teachings of Buddha. Those books are the new source of her awakening. Shivan could see her inclination to this new spirituality. Though he finds it is "excessive," he cannot stop seeing the change that it has brought in her life. She is no more "her old self" (Ibid, 293). And, this change makes him "envious" of her. She seems to be more patient, silent, forgiving, kind, accommodative, and receptive. She herself could not name this change, though she could see dimly its makers—those awful temporary jobs, her attempted suicide, the years of anger, departures of her children, the visit to the meditation centre, and the recent simple diet (Ibid). She had visited her ailing mother in Sri Lanka. Shivan remembers "the resonance" in her voice when she told him about her voyage: "I must do my duty" (Ibid, 296). During the visit, she makes peace with her mother and manages to undo the enmity between them to the extent that finally, Hema becomes the only solace to her mother. Shyam writes this peace-building between mother and daughter as follows:

> The day before her departure, my mother, Hema, said to her mother, as they had their breakfast together in her bedroom, "Amma, I would like you to dress nicely tomorrow morning. I want to take your photograph on the verandah before I go."
>
> "But why do you want a photograph, duva?" my grandmother complained. "Take any old one of me out of an album. I don't wish to be remembered as I am now."
>
> My mother didn't say anything. [...]
>
> "But no matter bad karma. I know now that I brought some very good karma from a previous life to this one. Yes-yes, I must have done something of great merit in a past existence to get a daughter like you, duva. Like rain soaking a parched land you are to me, like rain on parched land."
>
> [...]
>
> When it was finally time to leave the next day, she knelt in front of my grandmother's chair and, in the traditional way, touched her feet.
>
> My grandmother drew her daughter up and took her face in trembling hands. "Rattaramduva, the house will be bereft without you. Promise me you will return."
>
> "I will, Amma, I will."
>
> (Ibid, 295–296)

Her effort to make peace with her mother has enabled some inner peace within. It has given some strength to her not only to bear her mother but also her own self whom she could not bear, especially when she saw her mother in a dream. She kept seeing the same two dreams. In one, she saw her mother walking in her usual brisk manner ahead of her. When she called to her, she did not hear her; when she got hold of her, she did not know who she was and apologetically told her that she did not have a daughter called Hema. In the other dream, which was the "worse," she saw herself walking past the Wellawatte market and her mother was sitting outside the market begging, her skin covered with sores. She bent to reason with her, but her mother turned her head away (Ibid, 124–125). The second dream hurt her, making her wonder if her mother lost her mind or was "just angry" for being "abandoned" by her (Ibid, 125).

Though the death of her husband disallowed her to make peace with him by asking forgiveness for her anger, she at least realized her blunder—anger and hate. Force of anger and hate had disempowered her. It could give her nothing, but sucked all her energies which could have otherwise been channelized to earn calmness, peace, tranquillity, solace, and freedom *within*. Consequently, she was exhausted to the extent that she could not bear anyone, including herself. This aversion bursts in public on the first day to the meditation centre, making a public display of the aggression and impatience rising against others. It stopped her *listen*[10] to the sermon on The Four Limitless Qualities. Yet, she could hear some of it. What she heard had affected her unconsciously and begun to return to her after leaving the centre. It is this effect of what she heard that helps her later to realize the very cause of her suffering and pain—anger. Her anger was not only with others but also with herself. This most needed understanding helps her find a way to liberate herself from the anger that she had towards her mother and her husband. Her anger against them is pointless. She is the one who enacted all her past actions following her heart. In that sense, she should be angry with *her*. And, she *is*.

This realization of Hema is already a necessary step towards non-violence via freedom from anger. Yet, as Shyam writes, it is not adequate, because there is still some anger, which hinders Hema's liberation from suffering. Now, the writer takes us to yet another level concerning human anger, appealing us to think whether anger, hate, or any such vile feeling could be allowed within being against its (own) being since it does not harm any other being. Here, taking the Buddhist path for self-liberation, Shyam emphasizes the urgency of eradicating self-anger and self-hate since it does violence to the one within. He takes Hema on a spiritual journey that slowly detaches her from *her* being so that she *comes* to her as an outsider or (an)other. There, she becomes aware that her anger with herself is *actually* with yet another—another Hema, who is different from the one in the present. Yet, that difference does not allow her to undo her relation to the previous. She is related to her, yet differently. The deep self-enquiry of anger and hate delivers Hema to build a different relationship with the same being, unfolded differently throughout history. Then, if she remains angry with *that* Hema, she ends up becoming angry with the present one, different as well as, differently related to the same. There is no room to reject that difference in being who is called Hema. The being in Hema could appear only in difference. And it is the room in her for difference, which could deliver her to the being in the present. The Sermons heard at the Buddhist meditation centre and the texts, which she read, motivate her to make peace with the past.

In the question of making peace with the past as a way to manage anger and hate, Shyam intervenes in a commendable manner by proposing a long-lasting remedy through forgiveness. It is both a response and a remedy to the call of anger and hate. However, this is no easy task because forgiveness is always to come from the other. It is not some right that one could struggle to win. At the most, one could only plead or *beg* forgiveness from the other—the victim. It is only the victim who could forgive. Therefore, forgiveness is never *my* choice but the decision of the other.

Forgiveness always remains *to be* granted, for it can never be granted in one go. In forgiveness, one should go on *for-giving*—infinity. Philosophizing the idea of forgiveness, Jacques Derrida (2001c) emphasizes the "impossibility of forgiveness." As he argues, it is impossible to forgive because one does not know how to forgive the unforgivable. He says one does not forgive the forgivable.

Let's try to understand this puzzle.

If the one, who asks for forgiveness makes the request with the awareness that he/she *could be* forgiven for the injury done by him/her, forgiveness becomes something predictable or expectable to the one at the side of the request. If forgiveness remains as a possibility predictable to the one who asks for it, the discourses empowered by the idea of forgiveness—ethics, love, life, liberation, and freedom—become meaningless. That is why Derrida differentiates forgiveness from "judicial justice" (Ibid, 43). Justice is not forgiveness. It is outside justice. Yet, it is related or applicable to the discourse of (in)justice, for one could forgive only for something (some act done by someone), which can no way be justified—the act that does not deserve justice of any kind, the unpardonable. However, this decision *to forgive* or *not to forgive* bears, as Derrida argues, "the secret," which "juridico-political cannot approach" (Ibid, 55) but should be respected.

At any rate, forgiveness is not a discourse of power—the power of the powerful—or reason of the strongest (Ibid, 59). It is instead a discourse of the victim, the helpless or the vulnerable—the weaker in strength or power. The act of forgiving is an act that is to be born from the side of the weakest. It is only the victim who *could* forgive. However, being the only one capable of granting forgiveness, the victim—the powerless—*suddenly* becomes the strength—force—that could surpass the power by which he/she was victimized. In that sense, forgiving requires more force and strength than the power needed to harm, hurt, or wound another. That is why, Gandhian idea of forgiveness, which he terms as "a heritage that India can share with the world" (*All Men Are Brothers*, http://www.mkgandhi.org/amabrothers/almenarebrothers.htm, 65) is appealing to any discussion concerning forgiveness, which is, as Derrida would say, "worthy of its name."[11]

Gandhian idea emphasizes the strength of the one who forgives. "Forgiveness is the attribute of the strong" (Ibid, 192). This aspect emphasizes that forgiveness could only be a *deliberate* attempt. It does not come on its own. It does not happen or occur like how anger, hate, love, or jealousy happens. It has to be attempted intentionally. Victim needs to have the *intention* to forgive the one who harmed him/her. Here, the victim seems to be thinking: *Look, I know that you have harmed me. I am injured and I am in pain. Even if you apologize for what you have done to me, it cannot undo my pain. However, now, it is my turn and, I am capable of vengeance and inflicting pain on you. But, I do not want to exercise my power to hurt you since I am aware that pain is unbearable. This awareness from within tells me that I should not repeat vengeance and get into the cycle of pain and suffering. I should break free from the same. And I could do it* only *by freeing you from the pain that I could, otherwise, inflict upon you. Hence, I refrain from harming you. Now on, I for-give you that which no one else could give you—forgiveness.*

In the attempt of forgiveness, the victim slowly frees (its) being becoming the source of the pain or the suffering of another. However, this attempt is to be taken forward in and through some *inner* battle constantly going on within being. Accordingly, on the one side, there comes a question supported by certain presumptions: *Why should you forgive the unforgivable? You are stupid. If you forgive, the culprit neither would learn a lesson nor would he/she understand the gravity of the deed. Your forgiveness could only grant another chance for the culprit to do further damage to you or another. All the more, forgiveness cannot undo the past. Hence, don't forgive.*

On the other hand, there comes a thought that persuades being to forgive: *You should forgive only the unforgivable. It is true that you have all the power to withhold yourself from forgiving. It is solely up to you to decide whether to forgive or not. If you decide to not forgive, the culprit would be punished, and the punishment could be anything, including the death sentence. Thus, you are capable of murder—the ability to take the life of another. But, you are also capable of giving life to another. As far as giving life is concerned, you are the* only *one who could give that which should not be given. You are the only one capable of giving to the one who is not worthy of receiving anything from YOU. By becoming the power untransferable to another at this juncture to forgive or not forgive, you may decide how you would want to channelize it. Depending on how it is being channelled, you may either harm or save someone.*

Accordingly, the decision of forgiveness should emerge from the crucial point of contradictory forces pressing against each other. Shyam lays out this difficult condition, which being faces in a context concerning forgiveness, by writing down Shivan's inner battle regarding forgiveness for his grandmother. However, while writing (about) the impossible forgiveness operative beneath each attempt to forgive, he throws some light on how this entire exercise becomes tougher in the case of the following situations: One is, how could one be forgiven if the victim is no more alive? As Shyam writes, Hema's desire for forgiveness is met with such destiny, for the victim of her anger—her husband—is already dead, and the death of the victim disenables granting of forgiveness, even if it does not stop the culprit from pleading for forgiveness. The other is, how could one be forgiven even when forgiveness is not requested for?

The writer's remedy appears through Hema's suggestion to Shivan, burning with anger and hate towards his grandmother. According to him, Shivan is unable to forgive her for the thing which she did to Mili, especially because she is not ready to take responsibility for Mili's death.

"Has she accepted responsibility for what happened?"

"Whether she accepts responsibility or not isn't the issue. The issue is —"

"Only time will heal what happened, and as you see, it is already doing that." I held out my arms to show proof.

"Time isn't enough, you must also forgive."

"How can you forgive someone who hasn't taken responsibility for their actions?"

"*You start by forgiving yourself, that's where you start.*" [*Italics* mine]

"What should I forgive myself for? Did I kill Mili? Did I? Is that what you think?"

[...] I went to the top of the stairs. "Nothing can fix that, nothing can reverse her actions. It's too late to make any—"

"No, no, enough of your anger." She stood up. "I won't pander to it anymore."

(Selvadurai 2013, 329)

Here, what Shyam emphasizes is the *urgency* of forgiveness. And, it should come from within in the sense that one should start it with oneself. He writes, "You start by forgiving yourself, that's where you start." In that sense, forgiveness is first of all one's responsibility to its *own* self. So long as it appears as an irrepressible need, which one should address for one's own peace, solace, or freedom, one could always attempt to find a way to go about it. Nonetheless, the problem is, whether one remembers such a thing called forgiveness when one is self-obsessed and tries to maintain self-sameness in the strict sense. As Shyam writes, even if people are longing for peace, freedom, and happiness, they do not know how to attempt any of them without subscribing to some form of violence against someone or something. From the individual to communities, there is a tendency of agreeing with violence to bring peace or freedom. It is a strategy for peace: "war for peace" (Ibid, 147). Such *quick-fix* peace-building does not encourage any effort ruminating on forgiveness through *self-initiative withdrawal* from the harmful use of power.

Accordingly, forgiveness is not only about valuing life by gifting a chance to live but also withdrawing from a certain way of thinking and living—being. The withdrawal is not about absolute disengagement from power but refraining from certain ways of using power. Therefore, forgiveness is not a discourse, which proposes the urgency of rejecting or opposing power but one that reminds us of various possibilities of using power not to punish, harm, hurt, or destroy life but to care, respect, and save it. It is thus a critique not of power but the *application* of power—*ab-use* of power. And this sincere concern about the usability of power could begin only by calling the self into question so that one could realize how it has consciously or unconsciously used its power throughout the past and how both self and the other got affected by the same. It is only then one could see his/her mistakes and take responsibility for those past actions. Such an acceptance and undertaking on past is necessary to ponder on other ways of wielding power here-after—now and later. Shyam terms this deliberation as making peace with one's past, which, in his view, is an initiative for a peaceful future—a future free from hate and vengeance. Then, Hema's advice to Shivan on forgiveness is a direction for a peaceful future—a future *to come*. It is true, what *to come* is beyond the control of being, for it is *to come*, anyway. Yet, Shyam insists on tapping into some inner ability capable of empowering every human to face the future. That is the ability *to hope*. Everyone could hope. Accordingly, even if being is unable to have control over what to come as future, it, from its side, could expect that future to be better. Nevertheless, as he presents, this expectation is conditioned by what is being done in the present—*now* and *here*. Here, the writer emphasizes the Buddhist idea of *karma*, which encourages every being to do good *karma* in the present to take care of the future. Then, everyone could expect their future to be better ONLY IF they attempt to do good in the present.

Hema's difference, which, in turn, makes her a different Hema from the previous one, is testimony to this *karmic* effect. Her new way of life moves her along with the quotations from *A Guide to the Bodhisattva's Way of Life* in her mind. One such quote is as follows: "*WHEN THE MIND BURNS WITH ANGER, immediately cast aside those angry thoughts or they will spread the way an unchecked fire travels from house to house*" (Ibid, 43). And, she keeps *vigil* on her mind while working as well as walking for freedom and peace. Her efforts, along with constant attention to her mind, inform us that peace and freedom could be invented only through working on one's own mind constantly. Neither peace nor freedom could come on its own because there is no such thing, already defined as peace or freedom. They do not exist *as such* but to be invented at every moment, when one is unable to bear the other—the life in the relationship between self and the other. This invention is possible only by deconstructing what has already been invented—the self and the *I* language. They both are inventions in/through language, for language is capable of inventing when the things already invented become inadequate—inadequate to think, to understand, to accommodate, to accept, to express, and to survive the other.

Shyam is in the process of inventing in and through writing. He goes on inventing being for peace, as well as peace for being. His writing is suggestive of different possibilities of inventing being and inventing peace, also freedom. One of such ways could be through war or violence. As he writes, Chandrika's government had tried the strategy of "war for peace" in Sri Lanka. However, Shyam doubts whether peace could be invented through war. Even if it could be, for how long? After all, could there be any peace if it is found through violent and destructive means? Peace through war could nourish only enmity, hate, and vengeance from within, enabling further war and violence in the future. Shivan has already heard about such circulation of violence, caused by hate and vengeance, through a *Jataka* story narrated by his grandmother. It is the story of "The Demonness Kali." He still remembers how the story begins with the following line: *As a forest fire raging out of control only stops when it reaches a lake or river, so hatred and vengeance can only be quenched by the waters of compassion* (Ibid, 260).

The story in the novel thus begins with the message, which it intends to communicate. The whole purpose of telling this story is to convey the message that calls for compassion against hatred and vengeance. It has been told and passed on from one generation to another for centuries. That is how it had come to Shivan's grandmother. But, in the novel, it is Shivan who tells the story while saying he heard it from the grandmother. Shivan's story is placed before us by Shyam. Now, Shyam's way of saying it makes the story significant to the present-day context where evil unfolds in such unimaginable forms. As mentioned earlier, *Jatakas* could be read and re-told by anyone anywhere. However, the effect that it could make solely depends on *how* it is said. Its applicability or relevance in the day-to-day life of an individual as well as of a community is decided by how it is said. Shyam brings in this story while writing (about) the hate and enmity growing from within being against another being. This being is not only of the individual but also of the community. Accordingly, there is hate, anger, enmity, and vengeance, on the one hand, between mother and daughter, grandson and grandmother, husband and wife, children and parents, etc., and on the other hand, between Sinhalese and Tamils, the Sri Lankan army and the Liberation of Tamil Eelam (LTTE), left political parties and right political parties, whites and blacks, and so on. Shyam does not give importance to discussing *where* all hate, enmity, and anger could occur because it could happen anywhere with anyone. As Shivan's life unfolds in relation to others, we are convinced of the possibility of such forces appearing in any context. Such emotions know no categorical difference constructed by humans for themselves—universal. Hence, the focus should be on how to find a solution for this universal problem. Shyam insists on finding a solution that could sustain for long—perpetual peace. In his view, a long-term solution is possible only through a sincere effort initiated *to forgive*. As discussed above, the discourse of peace through forgiveness could begin only from the side of the victim of power—the other, the other side, the affected, or the harmed. Now, the story of "The Demonness Kali" talks about such kind of an attempt for peace through forgiveness. Shyam rewrites this old story with the words that come to him in writing (Ibid, 260–261). So doing, he presents what Buddha said to the demonness as follows:

> Listen, demonness, if your body is unclean with spit and phlegm and snot, can you use more spit and phlegm and snot to clean it? In the same way, you cannot use vengeance to cleanse a past wrong. No, it is only the waters of compassion that can cleanse your past enmities.
>
> (Ibid, 261)

Apart from the destructive side of anger and vengeance communicated in and through the story, Shyam, by (re)writing the story, underscores another deeper aspect that lies beneath the same. That is why I say that it is not the story *as such*, which matters to writing but the act of writing. In writing, a story unfolds uniquely, even if it has been narrated before by many others and is popular. The story of "The Demonness Kali" is popular in Sri Lanka, especially among Sinhala Buddhists. Like any other *Jataka* story, it is also narrated *as* a story in order that someone learns something from it and applies it in his/her life *whenever* necessary. It is thus used as a way to teach and guide people for a better life. Now, in Shyam's work, the story appears differently. There, it is not *only* a story that stands outside life so that life could be differentiated from the story. Instead, it is very much a part of life that unfolds *like* a story, yet not a story but more than a story. It appears within the writing while writing—being. It influences writing while becoming a part, which goes into creating the work—writing. Therefore, while writing it, the writer intervenes in it in a way, even the popular story becomes a creation of the one who writes it. Accordingly, the story of "The Demonness Kali" that comes in *The Hungry Ghosts* is one told by Shyam with his intervention. He intervenes in the story by telling it through writing. It is through this interruption-cum-intervention that he manages to bring certain aspects that lie beneath the story to the surface. And it is the aspect of *dharma,* which he proposes as a remedy to hate, anger, and vengeance. So doing, he underlines the story as that which not only could put forth the question of hate and vengeance but also could carry the remedy for the same *within*.

The *Jataka* story, intertwined with the one that is unfolding through writing, conveys the urgency of a third person—the other, who could intervene among those who fight against each other due to hate and anger. Any such context, constructed through perspectives appeared in language in terms of *I* and *You*—the first person and the second person—operates, enabling the structure of subject and object, in which one is positioned in opposition to the other, in which one is caught in one's *own* perception about itself as well as about the other. Here, both see each other in their point(s) of view(s), which is always *a* point of *I*: *I* see myself, *I* see you, *I* see myself in relation to you, and *I* see you in relation to myself. In each seeing, one ends up seeing one's (own) reflection. Such seeing could only give *my* vision or *my* knowledge—myself— back to me. Return of the same in returning to the same cannot bring or introduce something different to already existing enmity, hate, anger, and vengeance. Consequently, there would only be further anger, hate, and enmity. Then, there should be another domain outside I and You—third space or person—other.[12]

The third person or space is neither mine nor is it yours. It is some other who is able to see, observe, or watch both I and You in a neutral or non-align manner. Thus, it is always outside the domain of the two, positioned as the strong and the weak, subject and the object. The *Jataka* story shows us how these positions could inter-change and how the weaker becomes the stronger and vice versa with the shift of power. However, the mere shift of power cannot stop violence. It continues despite the shift until unless someone or something other than *this* power intervenes in it. In the story, it is Buddha who intervenes and interrupts the cycle of violence occurring due to anger and hate. He is able to see that both women are not able to see their (own) selves—the ignorance. He enlightens them by preaching *dhamma*. In Shyam's take on the story, Buddha's *dhamma* is about non-violence through compassion. Accordingly, it is the *dhamma* of non-violence through compassion which not only could save the child but also could liberate or redeem the two women caught up in the vicious circle of hate and enmity.

Nonetheless, the context in writing, within which the story of the demonness Kali appears, is one far from Buddha's time. Hence, there is no way that Buddha himself could intervene and enlighten those, who are fighting against each other for their desired ends. As Shyam notes, there is yet another way through which Buddha makes his appearance and intervention—*dhamma*. *Dhamma* is the legacy that he left behind so that it could appear in his absence to guide all beings for *nirvana*—freedom, happiness, and peace. Shyam celebrates *dhamma* as the *third* or the other space outside power, which desires to invade, subject, and rule the other. He writes how *dhamma* influences Shivan to initiate a mission for peace by forgiving himself in connection to all that had happened from him to another.

Freedom, Religion, and Literature

Considering the idea of freedom that appears in and through *The Hungry Ghosts*, it is of two kinds. One is what the writer is trying *to write*. The other is the one that is *getting written* in the act of writing. Accordingly, the first is connected to religion—Buddhism. Shyam offers to write the Buddhist idea of freedom, happiness, and peace, insisting on the Buddhist idea of non-violence through the practice of compassion, in which he projects freedom as something that needs to be earned by being through de-attachment to the self. The key to success in this mission is the renouncement of the desire for belonging. He conveys this message through the characters that he creates in writing. Each of them comes to this realization through their inner journeys to themselves, in which they realize the impermanence of being as the only truth. It is that truth, which leads them to change their approaches to life, love, freedom, happiness, and peace. In that sense, *The Hungry Ghosts* is a work of literature that celebrates the Buddhist idea of freedom through non-violence. The writer insists on the utmost relevance of the same to address a complex situation of power and violence that would erupt in Sri Lanka after the 1980s, engulfing the entire island in blood and tears. However, though he upholds its territorial integrity, his concern is not much on how to claim it and own it as a Sinhalese or Tamil but what happens to its people in each attempt to claim for the ownership by holding onto one's (own) desire, which either could be the desire of an individual or could it be of a community.

Beneath the Buddhist idea of freedom written and proposed in and through the novel, there is another freedom that *emerges* through writing. This freedom is *beyond* the writer's intention. Instead, it is what the work of language is capable of offering as a work, which is free from the one who created it. Work, as a creation in and through language through writing, does not belong to the one who wrote it. The writer has no control over what he has written (Blanchot 1995a). Though he desires to own the work by controlling the meaning that he wants it to carry, he cannot have such control over the same, since it is a work of language in which language takes the entire liberty of acting on its own and thus being able to be free from the creator. It is capable of survival without the one who made it. As mentioned in the early chapters, Blanchot always had fears about the liberty of language, though he had no way out other than falling back on the same, which could always leave him ruthlessly. Then, in writing, the writer is trying to own the language by capturing it. S/he tries to master it by enslaving it; makes use of it in her/his way to express what s/he wants. S/he writes, creates, expresses, and lives in and through language. Therefore, writing is a moment *of* language, as well as a moment *in* language, which is present only at the moment of writing—a moment in the present captured in and through language, *now* and *here*. It is at this moment of *now* and *here*, therefore, *nowhere*, that the writer is able to have control over that, which makes him/her a creator—language and the work. Once s/he stops or takes a break from writing, language, which was under his/her clutch, jumps out and begins to act freely. In that sense, every work of language through writing—literature—is open to a life, which is different from the one expected by the creator of the same. Derrida, therefore, compares this liberty of a work of language—a text—to that of a child, who steps out from the space under parental care and never comes back as the same. He upholds this character common to both child and text as follows:

> It's better to produce texts that leave and don't come back altogether, but that are not simply and totally alienated or foreign. One regulates an economy with one's texts, with other subjects, with one's family, children, desire. They take off on their own, and one then tries to get them to come back a little even as they remain outside, even as they remain the other's speech.
>
> (1985, 157)

Therefore, a text is like a child for "child is not only that toward which or for which a father or mother remains; it is an other who starts talking and goes on talking by itself, without your help" (Ibid).

The work as language, coming without the writer, could be accessed by anyone who takes an interest in it with the attempt of reading it. In each attempt to read, the reader writes it in his/her (own) way by (re) naming and (re)defining what is already named and defined in another language, as well as in another's language—idiom. Thus, in attempting to read a work of language, one tries to appropriate other's language yet in one's (own) way (DeArmitt 2014, 91–140; Derrida 1998). However, this always remains as an attempt without ever being able to succeed, for, as discussed in the previous chapter, language neither could be owned nor could be absolutely appropriated by anyone. Thus, it always remains to be approached, read, defined, and understood, despite all attempts already taken in relation to the text. This openness of/in language not only produces, as Derrida argues, "other ears, in a certain way—ears that I don't see or hear myself, things that don't come down to me or come back to me" (1985, 156), but also welcomes what to come, unconditionally—the future.

Then, this freedom exercised by a work of language—literature—cannot be reduced to one that is preached by any religion *as such*. Yet, it could be applied to any religion in order to understand the openness of every religion to outside—the future. Every religion, like a work of language, is open to anyone who likes to come to it or approach it by entering it in his/her *own* way. This singular entrance delivers being to the same religion in a different way, which, in turn, transforms the both—the one who enters religion and the one that welcomes the entry in passivity. Shyam is one such who finds his way in and through writing to approach Buddhism. In writing, both are being transformed by each other like the language in writing in which both the writer and the language are influenced and transformed by each other. Nevertheless, this singular attempt to approach Buddhism does not deliver him to Buddhism but to (an)*other* being invented in the process of trying to approach Buddhism, which, in turn, becomes the locus where (an)*other* Buddhism unfolds.

Notes

1 The idea of the strongest mentioned here is referred to the one discussed by Jacques Derrida in *The Politics of Friendship* where he examines the idea of the sovereign analyzed by Carl Smith. See Jacques Derrida, *The Politics of Friendship*, tr. G. Collins (London: Verso, 1997).

2 Mahatma Gandhi's ideas on civilization and freedom in *Hind Swaraj* are of utmost relevance here, as they emphasize the flaws of every civilization and freedom. See Mahatma Gandhi, *Hind Swaraj* or *Indian Home Rule* (Ahmedabad: Navajivan, 2000).

3 See Makarand R. Paranjape's critical perspectives in *Debating the "Post" Condition in India: General Vernaculars, Unauthorised Modernities, Postcolonial Contentions* (Abingdon: Routledge, 2018).

4 Discussing the idea of "colourful cosmopolitanism," Makarand Paranjape suggests how both West and East could co-create knowledge and spaces without trying to impose one over the other by creating a hierarchy. Here, one of the points that he highlights is the prevalence of differences in terms of cultures and traditions which in turn offers "different way of being in the world, with cultural exchange and circulation between 'coloured' or non-white populations and nations and horizontal and non-hierarchical modes of mutuality as opposed to vertical domination–subordination relations that marked the epoch of colonial expansion." See Makarand R. Paranjape, *Cultural Politics in Modern India: Postcolonial Prospects, Colorful Cosmopolitanism, Global Proximities* (London: Abingdon, 2016), 2.

5 Maurice Blanchot deals with this idea of death in most of his philosophical and literary works. See Maurice Blanchot, *The Work of Fire* tr. Charlotte Mandell (California: Stanford University Press, 1995a); *The Step Not Beyond* tr. Lysette Nelson (Albany: State University of New York Press, 1992); *The Writing of the Disaster* tr. Ann Smock (London: University of Nebraska Press, 1995b); "Thomas the Obscure," in *The Station Hill Blanchot Reader: Fiction & Literary Essays*, ed. George Quasha, tr. Lidiya Davis et al. (Barrytown: Station Hill Press, 1999), 55–28.

6 See Makarand R. Paranjape's discussion on self-restraint as Indian way of living in *Debating the "Post" Condition in India: Cultural Vernaculars, Unauthorised Modernities, Postcolonial Contentions* (Abingdon: Routledge, 2017).

7 See how Makrand R. Paranjape invents this term in *Another Cannon: Indian Texts and Traditions in English* (London: Anthem Press, 2009), 3.

8 Makarand R. Paranjape discusses the idea of "ways" of seeing and "ways" of being with reference to Indian tradition(s). See "Regaining the Indian Eye/I: The *rasas* of India," in *Cultural Politics in Modern India: Postcolonial Prospects, Colourful Cosmopolitanism, Global Proximities* (Abingdon: Routledge, 2017), 52–71.

9 See Derrida's critique on the formulation of this question itself in which he underscores how it presupposes the presence of self *as such*. Jacques Derrida, *Margins of Philosophy* tr. Alan Bass (Sussex: The Harvester Press, 1982), 51.

10 See Derrida's discussion on the difference between "being-heard" of the sound and the "sound-heard" in *Of Grammatology*, tr. Gayatri Spivak (Delhi: Motilal Banarsidass Publishers, 1994), 63.

11 Here, what Derrida attempts to propose is "forgiveness without power: unconditional but without sovereignty." However, it is important to note that Derrida's discussion on forgiveness underlines certain Abrahamic "heritage" that runs beneath the idea of forgiveness in the context of Europe, which he differentiates from the other ideas on the same, which are non-European and non-Abrahamic.

The idea of power is associated with the European idea of sovereignty, and it is different from the idea of "strong" that is explained by Gandhi in the context of forgiveness. For better understanding on both, see Jacques Derrida, *On Cosmopolitanism and Forgiveness*, tr. Mark Dooley and Michael Hughes (London: Routledge, 2001c); Mahatma Gandhi, *All Men are Brothers: Life and Thoughts of Mahatma Gandhi as Told in His Own Words*, ed. Krishna Kripalani (Ahmedabad: Jitendra T. Desai), https://www.mkgandhi.org/ebks/AllMenAreBrothers.pdf .

12 Derrida discusses problematic of the idea of the other presented in the Levinasian essay, "Violence and Metaphysics" in which he examines "what does autre mean before its Greek determination as heteron, and its Judeo-Christian determination as autrui? See Jacques Derrida, *Writing and Difference* tr. Alan Bass (London: Routledge, 1978), 130–192.

REFERENCES

Amunugama, Sarath. *The Lion's Roar: Angarika Dharmapala and the Making of Modern Buddhism*. Sri Lanka: Vijitha Yapa, 2016.

Benjamin, W. *Illuminations*. London: Pimlico, 1999.

Berkwitz, Stephen C. "Resisting the Global in Buddhist Nationalism: Venerable Soma's Discourse of Decline and Reform," *The Journal of Asian Studies* 67, no. 1 (February 2008): 73–106.

Betts, Judith and Claire Higgins, "The Sri Lankan Civil War and Australia's Migration Policy Response: A Historical Case Study with Contemporary Implications," *Asia & the Pacific Policy Studies* 4, no. 2 (2017): : 272–285. https://onlinelibrary.wiley.com/doi/full/10.1002/app5.181

Blanchot, Maurice. *The Space of Literature*. Translated by Ann Smock. Lincoln: University of Nebraska Press, 1982.

Blanchot, Maurice. *Step Not Beyond*. Translated by Lysette Nelson. Albany: State University of New York Press, 1992.

Blanchot, Maurice. *Work of Fire*. Translated by Charlotte Mandell. California: Stanford University Press, 1995a.

Blanchot, Maurice. *The Writing of the Disaster*. Translated by Ann Smock. Lincoln: University of Nebraska Press, 1995b.

Blanchot, Maurice. *Awaiting Oblivion*. Translated by John Gregg. Lincoln: University of Nebraska Press, 1997.

Blanchot, Maurice. *The Station Hill Blanchot Reader: Fiction & Literary Essays*, edited by George Quasha, Translated by Lidiya Davis et al. Barrytown: Station Hill Press, 1999.

Borradaris, Giovanna, ed. *Philosophy in a Time of Terror: Dialogue with Jurgen Habermas and Jacques Derrida*. Chicago: The University of Chicago Press, 2003.

Brannigan, John et al. ed. *Applying: To Derrida*. London: Macmillan Press, 1996.

Butler, Judith. *Gender Trouble*. New York: Routledge, 1990.

Caputo, John D., ed. *Deconstruction in a Nutshell: A Conversation with Jacques Derrida*. New York: Fordham University Press, 1996.

Cixous, Helene and Susan Sellers. *Three Steps on the Ladder of Writing*. New York: Columbia University Press, 1993.

Cixous, Helene. *"Coming to Writing" and Other Essays*, edited by Deborah Jenson, translated by Sarah Cornell et al. Cambridge: Harvard University Press, 1999.

Cixous, Helene. *Stigmata: Escaping Texts*. New York: Routledge Classics, 2005.

Cixous, Helene. "The Laugh of the Medusa," *Signs* 1, no. 4 (1976): 875–893.

Crépon, Marc. *Murderous Consent: On the Accommodation of Violent Death*. Translated by Michael Loriaux and James Martel. America: Fordham University Press, 2019.

Davids, Rhys, ed. *The Mahavamsa Or The Great Chronicle of Ceylon*. Translated by Wilhelm Geiger. Amen Corner: Oxford University Press, 1912. https://ia800300.us.archive.org/26/items/mahavamsagreatch00geigrich/mahavamsagreatch00geigrich_bw.pdf

DeArmitt, Pleshette. *The Right to Narcissism: A Case for an Im-possible Self-Love*. New York: Fordham University Press, 2014.

Deleuze, Gilles and Felix Gauthari. *A Thousand Plateaus: Capitalism and Schizophrenia*. Translated by Brian Massumi. London: University of Minnesota Press, 1987.

Derrida, Jacques. *Speech and Phenomena and Other Essays on Husserl's Theory of Signs*. Translated by David B. Allison. Evanston: Northwestern University Press, 1973.

Derrida, Jacques. *Writing and Difference*. Translated by Alan Bass. London: Routledge, 1978.

Derrida, Jacques. *Margins of Philosophy*. Translated by Alan Bass. Sussex: The Harvest Press, 1982.

Derrida, Jacques. *The Ear of the Other: Otobiography, Transference, Translation*. Translated by Peggy Kamuf. New York: Schocken Books, 1985.

Derrida, Jacques et al. "A Number of Yes (Nombre de oui)," *Qui Parle: Silence and Intervention* 2, no. 2 (1988): 118–133, https://www.jstor.org/stable/20713732 .

Derrida, Jacques. *Cinders*, edited and translated by Ned Luckacher. London: University of Nebraska Press, 1991.

Derrida, Jacques. *Acts of Literature*, edited by Derek Attridge. New York: Routledge, 1992.

Derrida, Jacques. *Of Grammatology*. Translated by Gayatri Chakrovorty Spivak. Delhi: Motilal Banarsidass, 1994.

Derrida, Jacques. *The Gift of Death*. Translated by David Wills. Chicago: The University of Chicago Press, 1995a.

Derrida, Jacques. *On the Name*, edited by Thomas Dutoit, translated by David Wood et al. California: Stanford University Press, 1995b.

Derrida, Jacques. "By Force of Mourning," *Critical Inquiry* 22, no. 2 (1996): 171– 192.

Derrida, Jacques. *Politics of Friendship*. Translated by George Collins. London: Verso, 1997.

Derrida, Jacques. *Monolingualism of the Other or the Prosthesis of Origin*. Translated by Patrick Mensah. California: Stanford University Press, 1998.

Derrida, Jacques. *Of Hospitality: Anne Dufourmantelle Invites Jacques Derrida to Respond*. Translated by Rachel Bowlby. California: Stanford University Press, 2000.

Derrida, Jacques. *The Work of Mourning*, edited by Pascale-Anne Brault and Michael Naas. Chicago: The University of Chicago Press, 2001a.

Derrida, Jacques and Maurizio Ferraris. *A Taste for the Secret*, edited by Giacomo Donis, translated by Giacomo Donis and David Webb. Cambridge: Polity Press, 2001b.

Derrida, Jacques. *On Cosmopolitanism and Forgiveness*. Translated by Mark Dooley and Michael Hughes. London: Routledge, 2001c.

Derrida, Jacques. *Acts of Religion*, edited by Gil Anidjar. New York: Routledge, 2002a.

Derrida, Jacques. *Negotiations: Interventions and Intervenes, 1971–2001*, edited and translated by Elizabeth Rottenberg. California: Stanford University Press, 2002b.

Derrida, Jacques. *Ethics, Institutions, and The Right to Philosophy*, edited by Henry A. Giroux. Maryland: Rowman & Littlefield Publishers, 2002c.

Derrida, Jacques. *Sovereignties in Question: The Poetics of Paul Celan*, edited by Thomas Dutoit and Outi Pasanen. New York: Fordham University Press, 2005.

Derrida, Jacques. *Psyche: Invention of the Other: Vol. I*, edited by Peggy Kamuf and Elizabeth Rottenberg. California: Stanford University Press, 2007.

Devotta, Neil. "Control Democracy Institutional Decay, and the Quest for Eelam: Explaining Ethnic Conflict in Sri Lanka," *Pacific Affairs* 73, no. 1 (2000): 55–76.

Dube, S.N. *Cross Currents in Early Buddhism*. New Delhi: Manohar Publications, 1980.

Duncan, Ronald, ed. *Selected Writings of Mahatma Gandhi*. London: Faber and Faber Limited. https://www.mkgandhi.org/ebks/SWMGandhi.pdf .

Fernando, Laksiri. "April 1971 JVP Uprising: Not to Make the Same Mistakes," *Colombo Telegraphs*, April 2, 2013. https://www.colombotelegraph.com/index.php/april-1971-jvp-uprising-not-to-make-the-same-mistakes/

Flippi, Gian Giuseppe. Mrtyu: *A Concept of Death in Indian Traditions: Transformation of the Body and Funeral Rites*. New Delhi: D. K. Printworld, 1996.

Foucault, Michel and Maurice Blanchot. *Foucault-Blanchot*. Translated by Brian Massumi and Jefrey Mehlman. New York: Zone Books, 1987.

Foucault, Michel. *Discipline and Punish: The Birth of the Prison*. Translated by Alan Sheridan. London: Penguin Books, 1991.

Foucault, Michel. *Ethics: Subjectivity & Truth: Vol I*, edited by Paul Rabinow, translated by Robert Hurley. New York: The New York Press, 1997.

Gandhi, Mahatma. *All Men Are Brothers (Life and Thoughts of Mahatma Gandhi as Told in His Own Words)*, edited by Krishna Kripalani. Ahmedabad: Navajivan. https://www.mkgandhi.org/ebks/AllMenAreBrothers.pdf .

Gandhi, Mahatma. *Hind Swaraj or Indian Home Rule*. Ahmedabad: Navajivan, 2000. https://www.mkgandhi.org/ebks/hind_swaraj.pdf .

Gombrich, Richard and Gananath Obeyesekere. *Buddhism Transformed: Religious Changes in Sri Lanka*. Delhi: Motilal Banarsidass Publishers, 1988.

Guruge, Ananda, ed. *Return to Righteousness: A Collection of Speeches, Essays and Letters of the Angarika Dharmapala*. Ceylon: Ministry of Education and Cultural Affairs, 1965.

Heidegger, Martin. *Being and Time*. Translated by John Macquarrie and Edward Robinson. Oxford: Basil Blackwell, 1962.

Holt, John Clifford. *The Buddhist Visnu: Religious Transformation, Politics, and Culture*. New York: Columbia University Press, 2004.

Hoole, Rajan. *Sri Lanka: The Arrogance of Power: Myths, Decadence & Murder*. Jaffna: University Teachers for Human Rights, 2001.

Iyer, Raghavan, ed. *The Essential Writings of Mahatma Gandhi*. Delhi: Oxford University Press, 1991.

Jayatilleka, Dayan. *Long War, Cold Peace: Sri Lanka's North-South Crisis*. Colombo: Vijitha Yapa, 2014.

Joyce, James. "Araby," *Dubliners*, USA: Planet eBook. http://www.apsmhow.org/Library%20Portal/index_htm_files/Dubliners.pdf

Kamuf, Peggy. *Book of Addresses*. California: Stanford University Press, 2005.

Keerawella, Gaminini. *Security Dilemma of a Small State: Part Two: Internal Crisis and External Intervention in Sri Lanka*. New Delhi: South Asian Publishers, 1995.

Kemper, Steven. *The Presence of the Past: Chronicles, Politics, and Culture in Sinhala Life*. Ithaca: Cornell University Press, 1991.

Kaushal, Sanjay. "An Investigative Study of 'Radical Passivity' in Philosophical and Literary Discourses." PhD dis. Jawaharlal Nehru University, 2016.

Khair, Tabish. *Night of Happiness*. New Delhi: Pan Macmillan, 2018.

Lacan, Jacques. *Ecritus: A Selection*. Translated by Alan Sheridan. London: Tavistock, 1980.

Levinas, Emmanuel. *Totality & Infinity: An Essay on Exteriority*. Translated by Alphonso Lingis. Pennsylvania: Duquesne University Press, 1969.

Levinas, Emmanuel. *Otherwise than Being or Beyond Essence*. Translated by Alphonso Lingis. Netherlands: Kluwer Academic Publishers, 1991.

Manor, James. *The Expedient Utopian: Bandaranaike and Ceylon*. Cambridge: Cambridge University Press, 1989.

Menike, Nimmi Nalika. "Religion, Nation, and Gender: A Study of the Problematic of Representation and Violence in the Context of Sri Lankan Literature." PhD dis. Jawaharlal Nehru University, 2016.

Menike, Nimmi Nalika. "Love Beyond Body Offering: Literature and Generosity," *Journal of Human Values* 26, no. 3 (2020): 248–55.

Muffe, Chantal, ed. *Deconstruction and Pragmatism: Simon Critchley, Jacques Derrida, Ernesto Laclau & Richard Rorty*. London: Routledge, 1996. https://monoskop.org/images/0/06/Mouffe_Chantal_ed_Deconstruction_and_Pragmatism_1996.pdf

Munasinghe, Chamika. *Pujya Gangodavila Soma Himipanange Mage Deshaya Avadi Karana Handa*. Colombo: Dayawamsa Jayakody & Company.

Munaweera, Nayomi. *Island of a Thousand Mirrors*. Haryana: Hachette India Local, 2013.

Nalika, Nimmi. "The Hungry Ghosts: Self-identity in the Question of Love and Responsibility," *Asian Quarterly: An International Journal of Contemporary Issues* 16, no.4 (2019): 5–14.

Obeyesekere, Gananath. *The Buddha in Sri Lanka: Histories and Stories*. Abingdon: Routledge, 2018.

Ondaatje, Michael. *Anil's Ghost*. London: Bloomsbury Publishing Plc, 2000.

Paranjape, Makarand R. *Another Canon: Indian Texts and Traditions in English*. London: Anthem Press, 2009.

Paranjape, Makarand R. *Body Offering*. New Delhi: Rupa Publications, 2013.

Paranjape, Makarand R. *Cultural Politics in Modern India: Postcolonial Prospects, Colourful Cosmopolitanism, Global Proximities*. Abingdon: Routledge, 2017.

Paranjape, Makarand R. *Debating the 'Post' Condition in India: Cultural Vernaculars, Unauthorized Modernities, Postcolonial Contentions*. Abingdon: Routledge, 2018.

Perera, Indu. *Misaditu Bindina Handa: Pujya Gangodavila Soma Himi*. Colombo: Dayawamsa Jayakody & Company.

Perera, Sasanka. *The Ethnic Conflict in Sri Lanka: A Historical and Sociopolitical Outline*. Washington DC: World Bank, 2001. http://documents.wolrdbank.org/curated/en/727811468302711738

Raju, C.K. "Ending Academic Imperialism: ABeginning," http://ckraju.net/papers/Academic-imperialism-final.pdf

Ratnapalan, Laavanya M. "Memories of Ethnic Violence in Sri Lanka among Immigrant Tamils in the UK," *Ethnic and Racial Studies* 35, no. 9 (2012): 1–34. https://hal.archives-ouvertes.fr/hal-00713344.

Sadercock, Leonie et al., "The Quest for an Inclusive City: An Exploration of Sri Lanka Tamil Experience of Integration in Toronto and Vancouver," *Research on Immigration and Integration in the Metropolis (RIIM): Working Paper Series, Vancouver Centre of Excellence*, May, 2004. https://www.yumpu.com/en/document/read/33358835/the-quest-for-an-inclusive-city-metropolis-bc .

Sartre, Jean Paul. *Being and Nothingness: An Essay on Phenomenological Ontology*. Translated by Sarah Richmond. London: Methuen & Co., 1957.

Selvadurai, Shyam. *Funny Boy*. New Delhi: Penguin Books, 1994.

Selvadurai, Shyam. *Cinnamon Gardens*. Haryana: Penguin Books, 1998.

Selvadurail, Shyam. *Story-Wallah*. Canada: Thomas Allen Publishers, 2004.

Selvadurail, Shyam. *The Hungry Ghosts*. New Delhi: Penguin Books, 2013.

Selvadurai, Shyam, ed. *Many Roads through Paradise: An Anthology of Sri Lankan Literature*. Haryana: Penguin Books, 2014.

Shastri, Dakshinaranjan. *Origin and Development of the Rituals of Ancestor Worship in India*. Calcutta: Bookland Private Limited, 1963.

Soma, Gangodavila. *Deshaya Surakina Ran Asipatha*. Colombo: Dayawamsa Jayakody & Company.

Sophocles. *The Theban Plays*. England: Penguin Books, 1967.

Tambiah, Stanley J. *Buddhism Betrayed? Religion, Politics, and Violence in Sri Lanka*. Chicago: The University of Chicago Press, 1992.

Tambiah, Stanley J. *Sri Lanka: Ethnic Fratricide and Dismantling of Democracy*. Delhi: Oxford University Press, 1986.

Verma, Vidhu. ""Reinterpreting Buddhism" Ambedkar on the Politics of Social Action," *Economic and Political Weekly* 45, no. 49 (2010): 56–65. https://www.epw.in/journal/2010/49/special-articles/reinterpreting-buddhism-ambedkar-politics-social-action.html

Werake, Mahinda and P.V.J. Jayasekera, ed. *Security Dilemma of a Small State: Part Two – Internal Crisis and External Intervention in Sri Lanka*. New Delhi: South Asian Publishers, 1995.

Wilson, A. Jeyaratnam. *Sri Lankan Tamil Nationalism: Its Origins and Development in Nineteenth and Twentieth Centuries*. Vancouver: UBC Press, 2000.

INDEX

www.ingramcontent.com/pod-product-compliance
Lightning Source LLC
Chambersburg PA
CBHW071527100726
47908CB00004B/1310